IMAGINE THAT...
THE HISTORY OF
FOOTBALL
REWRITTEN

MICHAEL SELLS

Published in the UK in 2013 by
Icon Books Ltd, Omnibus Business Centre,
39–41 North Road, London N7 9DP
email: info@iconbooks.net
www.iconbooks.net

Sold in the UK, Europe and Asia
by Faber & Faber Ltd, Bloomsbury House,
74–77 Great Russell Street,
London WC1B 3DA or their agents

Distributed in the UK, Europe and Asia
by TBS Ltd, TBS Distribution Centre, Colchester Road,
Frating Green, Colchester CO7 7DW

Distributed in India by Penguin Books India,
11 Community Centre, Panchsheel Park,
New Delhi 110017

Distributed in South Africa by
Book Promotions, Office B4, The District,
41 Sir Lowry Road, Woodstock 7925

Distributed in Australia and New Zealand
by Allen & Unwin Pty Ltd,
PO Box 8500, 83 Alexander Street,
Crows Nest, NSW 2065

Distributed in Canada by
Penguin Books Canada,
90 Eglinton Avenue East, Suite 700,
Toronto, Ontario M4P 2Y3

ISBN: 978-184831-566-2

Typeset in New Baskerville by Simmons Pugh
Printed and bound in the UK by Clays Ltd, St Ives plc

Contents

Imagine that ...

Some of history's greatest stories are the tales of what might have been. The agonising missed chances, the harrowingly close shaves, the vital complications that affected a major outcome – the course of history is a precarious one. Seemingly insignificant incidents can have the largest unforeseen impacts.

Scientists have pondered whether the flap of a butterfly's wings on one continent could lead to a tornado on another, and these chains of cause and effect remain fascinating to us. In this book and the others in the series I take a look at those moments where the smallest tweak would have caused history to pan out very differently.

Hence the title, *Imagine That* ...

Michael Sells

Chapter 1

Imagine that ...

Substitutions are never introduced to football ... and the game is rid of greed and disloyalty

It was a change that transformed the game and brought with it a wealth of new footballing lingo: the benchwarmer, the tinkerman, the supersub, the tactical change, the last throw of the dice, the impact player. It brought a whole new dimension to a manager's job description and the game of football in general. The role and form of the substitution has come a long way in the years since its introduction over half a century ago.

Substitutions were first introduced by the International Federation of Association Football (FIFA) in 1953 in the run-up to the 1954 World Cup finals held in Switzerland. The qualifying stages were used as a test ground for the new idea, allowing teams to list twelve players in their match-day squad so that one player could be replaced should they receive an injury. There was obvious sense behind the idea. It meant that games would remain competitive provided that no more than one player from each team suffered injury, while removing the need for players to play on through serious injuries.

Twelve years later, on 21 August 1965, substitutions made their entrance on to the English domestic scene in a second-division fixture at Bolton's Burnden Park stadium. Only a few minutes of the match had passed when the goalkeeper for visiting side Charlton suffered an injury. He would have to come off. It was the moment the Football Association (FA) had been waiting for, a chance to see the new concept in action. There was one small problem, though; Charlton hadn't brought a substitute goalkeeper with them. Nevertheless, a substitution was made and midfielder Keith Peacock made his way on to the pitch as a reshuffle saw left-back John Hewie don the gloves. In rather predictable fashion, Bolton struck four past the makeshift keeper as the game finished 4–2, but Keith Peacock had cemented his place in pub quizzes for years to come. The scoreline, however, highlighted the fact that there were still a few issues to iron out.

At the end of the following season, in the summer of 1967, the FA decided that a change was needed and gathered to discuss how best to proceed. The headline decision was that substitutions would remain a part of English football. They provided a common-sense solution to an unavoidable problem. However, the first two seasons to have featured substitutes had not been without controversy – and in a manner far more worrying than Charlton's missing goalie. An element of gamesmanship had slowly crept into proceedings.

More and more injuries were occurring in seemingly innocuous situations, players apparently feigning injury under instruction so that they could be replaced. Suddenly the burden had fallen upon referees not only to spot fouls, but also to judge whether the resulting injuries were genuine. The FA decided that from the 1966/7 season onwards teams would be allowed to make substitutions for tactical reasons as well as due to injury. It was a turning point in football, representing the beginning of a more professional era. As in the earlier international matches, the substitutions ensured that teams would not be needlessly punished for their players' injuries, but also afforded managers a new level of control once games were under way. They could tinker with their formations, replacing a defender with a striker when they were losing and vice versa when they wished to protect a lead. The game was becoming a far more fluid entity, evolving over the course of each 90-minute match.

This is how it remained, on the domestic scene at least, for a couple of decades until towards the end of the 1980s when the Football Association began to tinker with the rules almost year upon year. In 1988 a period of great change in English football, and eventually worldwide, was nudged into action. It began with an increase in the number of substitutes allowed, from one to two, essentially increasing the match-day squad to thirteen. This made the latter stages of football matches far more competitive – depending of course upon what type of players the manager selected for the bench. There was still no ruling over substitute goalkeepers, so trembling outfield players pulling on oversized jerseys and gloves remained a common sight. Then, in 1992, the top division in England was renamed and reformatted. The First Division became the Premier League. Intended to give the English game a glossy new finish following a decade marred by violence and resultant exclusion from European competition, the emphasis was on excitement. It was the beginning of an effort to neatly package the game for television and this transition period reformed an abundance of aspects, from gameplay to financial structuring. Naturally, the subs bench received an update as a further spot was added, with clubs now allowed to name and use three substitutes. As the substitution rules altered, squad sizes swelled. Whereas in the 1960s and 70s squads were typically no more than fourteen or fifteen players strong, at the start of the Premier League era the average squad size was nearer to 25 or 30. With more spaces available in a match-day squad, it made sense to retain more players overall.

A couple of years later, at the start of the 1994/5 season, goalkeepers received a boost. It became mandatory for teams to include a substitute goalkeeper, a change that had been a long time coming and marked a return to the original purpose of substitutions: to keep games competitive. The change was short-lived, however, as the stipulation for a substitute goalkeeper to be named was dropped the following season. Football's focus had changed from competitiveness to drama.

Two seasons later the overhaul continued as clubs were allowed to name five substitutes, although still only three of these could be used in a match. This was the final change to substitute ruling for just over a decade until the bench size was increased to seven in 2008, at which size it currently remains. Although the changes seem small, their cumulative effect was significant. By 2004, international friendly matches had become a farce. The ruling on substitutions in international friendlies was far more relaxed than the domestic rulings and resulted in games like England's against Australia in 2003. The game was televised as well as being covered online in the form of text updates. The *Guardian* was one of the outlets covering the game via their website, and set the game up in underwhelming fashion:

> Welcome everyone to what will surely prove to be the most meaningless friendly in a long time. Sven-Goran Eriksson plans to make so many substitutions, the linesman's numbers board should ideally carry a strobe warning for epileptics.

The prediction proved to be spot on as Eriksson sent a completely different eleven out in the second half to the one which had started the first. The result was a disjointed performance that allowed Australia to claim their first-ever victory against England, by three goals to one. Far from the original intention of making games more competitive, substitutions were now devaluing and eradicating any sense of competition. FIFA acted to limit the number of subs in international friendlies to six, still showing lenience towards the experimental nature of the games, but the world of football is still struggling to manage the knock-on effects of the squad culture brought about by substitutions.

The current situation is by no means the extreme. Football could become even more of a squad game, and some influential figures would like to see this happen. At the start of the 2012 season new regulations came into play in Serie A, Italian football's top tier. The maximum number of substitutes that could be named was increased to twelve. The change was the result of lobbying from club presidents, most notably Aurelio de Laurentiis of Napoli. He outlined his thoughts on the matter afterwards, saying that 'it was unfair to send [squad] players to the stands as it threatened to see their value plummet. It [the rule change] proves it is not impossible to change the world of football, but we have stood still for too long.' It is certainly true that including a

fringe players among the substitutes allows a club to give the impression both to the player and to potential buyers that he is more important than he actually is.

Even so, the new arrangement is far from universally beneficial. The size of the bench allows clubs to arrive at matches with what is essentially an entire B team prepared to step in, but many teams do not have sufficient squad depth to do so. It benefits the heavyweights of the division, such as AC Milan, Internazionale, Juventus and de Laurentiis' Napoli, enabling them to assert their dominance over smaller opposition. As de Laurentiis also admitted, it enables clubs to inflate a player's value via match-day inclusion, a feat which further increases the financial gulf between the top teams and the chasing pack.

Club presidents may celebrate this change, but it contributes to the most damaging side-effect of the substitution: the increasing trend for players' worth to be judged by their

monetary value rather than by their footballing ability. The hoarding of players is a pandemic that has swept the top leagues of the world. Whether a club is holding on to excess players to maximise its match-day options, to prevent opposition teams from employing them or simply because it is rich enough to do so, the effect is always the same. Talent is wasted. Players fester on the sidelines, going through the motions each week in training with no real hope of breaking into the first team; it is a culture which breeds apathy and disillusionment. The only way clubs can keep the superfluous squad members happy is by paying them handsomely. While some will still argue that the world's greatest players deserve their astronomical contracts, few would advocate such wages for a benchwarmer, of which there are plenty.

One of the most pilloried beneficiaries of the squad system is Winston Bogarde. He enjoyed great success early in his career, including a Champions League win and two league titles with Ajax, and a further two Spanish titles and a domestic cup with Barcelona. These are impressive honours; indeed, to even play for such clubs is an achievement that many players can only dream of. This made the final chapter of Bogarde's career all the more troubling. He secured a transfer to English side Chelsea on a contract believed to be around £40,000 a week. Having played in the top divisions of Holland, Spain and Italy (managing a handful of games with AC Milan) it made sense for him to test his talents in another of Europe's elite leagues, but what followed was far from testing. With first-team opportunities at a premium during his four-year stay at Chelsea, other clubs began to sniff around. On approaching him, however, they usually received the same response PSV Eindhoven did in 2004: 'It would be great to play for PSV but only if they pay my full salary.' In the end Bogarde saw out his contract, making a measly eight starts and three substitute appearances during his four-year stay. This worked out at over £1 million in wages for every starting appearance.

With clubs acting like banks rather than sporting institutions, it is no wonder that for some players football itself has become a secondary interest. Nor is it any surprise that club loyalty has dwindled. In his autobiography, former Leeds United manager (1974–8) Jimmy Armfield spoke of contract negotiations with the club's long-serving player Paul Madeley. As was standard practice, Armfield began discussions with talk of wages but Madeley did not want to hear it. 'He replied that he had no intention of leaving Leeds,' said Armfield, 'so he might as well sign the contract and let me fill in the details.' There was no hint of careerism in Madeley's thought process, just undying loyalty. This tale gains greater significance in contrast to Bogarde's sorry stint at Chelsea when you consider Madeley's role at Leeds. He was nicknamed 'Mr Versatility', happy to appear in any position and fulfil any role for the club, making 711 appearances during his seventeen years at the club. In an era when positions were synonymous with shirt numbers, he wore seven different numbers in his nine different cup final appearances – only one shirt number fewer than Bogarde had starts.

It would be untrue to suggest that loyalty does not still have a place in football. Arsenal defender Tony Adams ech-

oed Madeley, saying: 'I will sign every contract Arsenal put in front of me without reading it.' Italy has produced a number of one-club players including Francesco Totti, Daniele de Rossi (both AS Roma) and Paolo Maldini (AC Milan). The core of Barcelona's record-breaking side has never played for another club, including the likes of Xavi, Andrés Iniesta, Victor Valdés and Carles Puyol. Small glimpses of loyalty can still be seen across football, but it is now seen as quirky for a player to spend their entire career at one club.

Football is a shorter career than most. The majority of players will sign their first contract at seventeen or eighteen and play until their early- to mid-thirties. All in all that amounts to little over a decade in the game, so arguably a slightly inflated wage during that time might be justified. But with competitive playing time limited to 90 minutes once, maybe twice, a week for eight or nine months a year, that decade begins to look a lot shorter. When you factor in the substitutes' bench, it becomes evident that there are many players who are paid handsomely to hone skills that they will use for only a few hours each year. Before substitutes were introduced, a squad would stand at around thirteen or fourteen players. That was to allow for a couple of replacements over the course of a season. As the number of allowed match-day substitutes increased, so too did the squad size. Up to a point this was sensible; injuries and suspensions made three or four reserve players a necessity. However, as match-day squads have increased to include seven or even twelve substitutes, the squads have increased out of all proportion. At the start of the English Premier

League's 2009/10 season, the teams' squad lists made for staggering reading. Two of the league's more traditionally successful outfits, Arsenal and Liverpool, had registered over 60 players each. Effectively that would enable them to field an entirely different first team in five consecutive games, far more players than any team needs to employ.

The knock-on effect is dramatic and suggests that Winston Bogarde was just the tip of the iceberg. Many of the players on the books of these Premier League clubs are full internationals, a large number of whom will settle for a handful of starts per season. These are players with the ability to cut it on the international scene but who instead are content to forfeit regular football for a hefty wage and a cushy lifestyle. However, other squad players are not international quality. Many are signed for the sole purpose of providing emergency back-up; strength in numbers. Although improvements in training and coaching techniques may have led to a rise in the overall standard of football and, in turn, more top-quality footballers, the number of truly great players has not increased five-fold. The players warming the benches and filling the training pitches of top-flight clubs are the players who 20 or 30 years ago would have been cult heroes at lower-league clubs. They would have been the iconic players that attract fans to those clubs with lesser means, providing a vital cash boost. Now, though, these clubs are priced out as the players hoard their money elsewhere. The mindset that it has engendered, one that has starved lower-league clubs of their stars, was so neatly summed up by none other than Winston Bogarde:

This world is about money, so when you are offered those millions you take them. Few people will ever earn so many. I am one of the few fortunates who do. I may be one of the worst buys in the history of the Premiership, but I don't care.

It is often difficult to grasp at first the true ramifications of new rules and concepts in football. Some rulings fade quickly out of use, but substitutions have edged further and further into football. What was once a simple solution to combat injuries is now the source of greedy, disloyal and disaffected footballers.

FIFA

or the Game. For the World.

Sepp Blatter

Chapter 2

Imagine that...

Goal-line technology clears up football's greatest debates ... and leaves fans disillusioned by an unjust sport

As the world strode bravely into the 21st century, embracing the accompanying advancements and technology, football's governing bodies looked on, unsure of how to adapt and displaying unmistakable symptoms of technophobia. Football clubs, on the other hand, have called almost unanimously for a technological upgrade. Gizmos and gadgets have managed to filter into individual clubs and even, quietly, some leagues which have then been held up as startling exceptions and ultra-progressive institutions. Since the turn of the century top-flight clubs have embraced the services of companies such as Prozone, a Leeds-based enterprise whose product enables coaches to digitally map the movements and per-formances of players for fitness monitoring and tactical use. Yet it has taken until 2013 for a major football association

to take the first steps towards installing goal-line technology, devices designed to determine whether a goal has or has not been scored. In April 2013 the chairmen of the English Premier League voted in favour of incorporating technology in time for the following season, a bold move with the potential to make up the minds of football associations across the world.

Goals are of course the most important aspect of any match, with victory and defeat gauged by how many times the ball crosses the line, so it was surely worth investing money in an accurate method of determining this, even if only to prove it wouldn't work. The technology in question has been available since 1999 so the problem is not one of invention. Devices such as the patented Hawk-Eye, the Premier League's technology of choice, were eagerly embraced by other sports such as cricket, tennis and rugby upon their availability and the pivotal moments in each respective sport are now, on the whole, correctly judged. Football, meanwhile, plodded on without. Speaking in 2005 at a commercial event, FIFA chief Sepp Blatter gave his thoughts on the matter:

> I would say we shall live with the errors, not only the errors of the players and the coaches but we shall also live with the errors of the referees. So, let the game be as it is.

His critics considered this to be a remarkably weak response and it failed to mute their discontent. Blatter's stance eventually softened, but only after a number of high-profile 'ghost goals' and disallowed match-winners.

It is not just those at the top of the footballing pyramid who have been averse to modernisation; many football 'purists' fear it will sap the high tempo that attracts so many to the game. The buzzword is 'momentum'. Those sports that have introduced technology are distinguishable by a common scene. Play stops as tens of thousands of fans turn their attention away from the pitch. The players and referee also turn away, fixing their gaze upon electronic scoreboards and awaiting confirmation. For the trickier decisions it can take minutes for a decision to be reached. All the while muscles are tightening and adrenaline is diminishing. The waiting game brought about by the giant scoreboards turns once fast-paced sporting battles into pantomime. IN! OUT! NOT OUT! TRY! NO TRY! The immediacy and raw emotion these events would usually hold is tempered by the agonising wait. Jubilation is replaced by relief; disappointment worsened by false hope. It is this sterility that the purists fear would harm the game, and the argument does have merit. The drama that accompanies indecision is part of the game. In some cases a poor decision may drive a set of supporters to despair but for the rest of us, the opposition and the neutrals, it provides a talking point, a source of debate.

According to sceptics, then, embracing this technology could easily reduce the fast-paced sport that is adored by so many to a stop-start quest for 100 per cent accuracy. One of

the technology's greatest detractors, UEFA chairman Michel Platini (pictured left), agrees. Platini said in 2012 of proposals to introduce the technology: 'It invades every single area. We can't just have goal-line technology. We also need sensors to see if someone has handballed it. We need cameras to see if it should be a goal or not.' Despite his somewhat intolerant rebuffing of the proposal, there was a great deal of truth to his argument. With a culture of technology implanted into football, it is highly possible that finer tweaks to include offside checks, replays to assess fouls in-game and other mooted uses will be inevitable. Platini's fears of opening the floodgates are by no means baseless, as the world of rugby has shown. Originally, the Television Match Official or 'video referee' was supposed to confirm to the on-pitch referee whether or not a player had scored a try. Gradually the TMO's duties have increased, to the point that the English Premiership has even trialled a system where the referee can request that the TMO rewinds the tape to spot infringements earlier in play. The video referee was intended to be a silent introduction to the game, aiming to seamlessly root out injustice, but it now does far more.

The refusal to accept technology into football is viewed by many as an archaic unwillingness to adapt, but there is something very human about the hesitancy. Football has existed and excelled until now without the need for mechanical intervention. One of the sport's greatest attractions is that it can be played anywhere. No other sport spans the globe with quite the same degree of universality as football, and that is largely due to the fact that

it requires no specialist equipment. You can recreate the events of a World Cup final by substituting some rolled-up socks or a spherical fruit for a ball; swapping boots for bare feet and a goal frame for a brick wall. But there is no natural replacement for video technology. It would mark a new era in football, with the professional game materially set apart from the one taking place in parks and streets worldwide. In spite of all the vitriol that overflows when a goal of vital importance is ruled out incorrectly, there is something quite admirable about the stance taken by FIFA. With football undertaking its first serious and prolonged trial of technology, the fact that the role of referees is only now being supplemented shows a touching dedication to the game; it is hard to attack inaction born out of almost childlike idealism.

Whether or not goal-line technology *should* have been introduced sooner, things would not have panned out in quite the same way if it had been. There are countless episodes from footballing history that could have been transformed by its presence. The 1966 World Cup, for example, could well have ended up in West German hands. With the final match of the tournament deadlocked at 2–2 after 90 minutes, bitter rivals England and West Germany entered 30 minutes of extra time. With tension rising and the clock ticking away, full-back Alan Ball crossed the ball to Geoff Hurst. With his back to goal, Hurst controlled the ball and turned before striking at goal, losing his balance as he did so. The German goalkeeper Hans Tilkowski instinctively raised a hand, appearing to tip the ball up on to the crossbar. The ball then thundered down towards the goal line before bouncing away. Players from both sides raised their arms to appeal: the English claiming a goal, the Germans denying it. This was not an act of gamesmanship and they were not attempting to fool the linesman. It is quite conceivable that both sides thought they were correct as, nearly 50 years on, debate continues over whether or not the ball crossed the line. It was too close to call in real time and still inconclusive when the videos were replayed. After giving a long puzzled look, the Azerbaijani linesman Tofik Bahramov awarded a goal. It looked very much like guesswork, but a decision had to be made. If the goal had been disallowed then the pattern of play would undoubtedly have altered, with the teams' emotions reversed. England, playing with freedom and jubilance, went on to score a fourth goal to clinch victory, but without the cushion of their third goal it could so easily have been Germany running out winners. As damaging as stopping a game to consult a video can be, allowing it to carry on with the momentum behind the wrong team is worse.

This is all hypothetical, of course. It would have been unfeasible for goal-line technology to have been used, such was the expensive and impractical nature of videography at the time. As much as the incident needed a definitive answer, it just would not have been possible without putting the game on hold indefinitely.

High-profile and pivotal games today are still full of these knife-edge moments. Long, drawn-out seasons so often boil down to one game. Teams play within themselves or exceed expectations relative to their nearest challengers. Sometimes this means title rivals heading into the final week of the season needing to better each other's results.

Sometimes it sees a cluster of sides frantically dropping in and out of relegation zones as goals fly in throughout the day. Other times, the all-important fixture is played midway through the season. In the case of the 2011/12 Serie A season in Italy, this is exactly what happened. When title challengers Juventus and AC Milan met on 25 February 2012 there was still plenty of football to be played. However, with Milan sitting atop the table and Juventus just a point behind with a game in hand, it was dubbed as a major battle in the seasonal war. Milan took the lead after fifteen minutes and continued to press. Twenty-five minutes in, they worked a short corner before Brazilian playmaker Robinho swung the ball into the box. Milan defender Philippe Mexes powered a header towards goal and, after Juventus goalkeeper Gianluigi Buffon had parried the effort, Ghanaian midfielder Sulley Muntari prodded the ball over the line.

Or so he thought. As Muntari and co wheeled off in celebration, the referee waved Buffon and Juventus to play on. Replays showed the ball to have been a foot or so over the line before Buffon had scooped it back into play. It mattered not: as the game continued, Juventus eventually equalised to take a point home to Turin. It was the turning point of the season. Instead of extending their lead, both in the game and in the league, Milan were pegged back by their rivals. A similar event followed a month later when they faced Catania: Robinho saw a perfectly good winner ruled out, and his side once again drew a game they might have won. A sense of injustice stirred within Milanese stomachs for the rest of the season. Milan's club president Adriano Galliani spoke about his anguish in an interview with Sky Sports Italia, saying: 'I carry the photos of Muntari's goal and Robinho's goal on my phone, but I look more often at Muntari's.' The two games proved to be pivotal, as the extra four points they would have gained from the respective victories (not to mention the point Juventus would have lost) saw Milan finish four points short. 'Ghost goals' had altered the outcome of a 38-game season.

Juventus also complained of injustice in other matches, and as the old adage goes, 'It all evens itself out over the course of the season', but should it have to? In 2012, amid a title race similar to that taking place in Serie A, Manchester City coach Patrick Vieira spoke out about the opposition's record with refereeing decisions. The team in question were Manchester United, their city and title rivals. With mind games played out in the media taking a prominent role in any English season, Vieira's outburst was not altogether surprising, and his point hardly a new one. In 2004 in a game between Liverpool and Manchester United at Old Trafford, a remarkable streak for United came to an end. Just after the hour mark Liverpool midfielder Steven Gerrard burst into the opposition penalty area, only to be brought down. The referee, Mike Riley, pointed to the penalty spot. That in itself was an unusual sight. Fellow midfielder Danny Murphy placed the ball on the spot and coolly dispatched his shot beyond Man U keeper Tim Howard. No sooner had the ball hit the net than sports statisticians were compiling their latest offerings for the broadcasters. The penalty was only the fourth to be awarded to the away side at Old Trafford in over a decade and the first to be scored. As this statistic made its way around the footballing world, many took it as confirmation of what they had long believed.

However, although the Old Trafford penalty drought was one of the more alarming spells in football – especially since the lack of penalties was not the result of a lack of seemingly valid claims – it is a trend that seems to benefit the sides with larger followings. In his own attack on the Old Trafford side, Patrick Vieira had been keen to stress that they were just one of many sides to benefit from favourable decisions.

I think when you go to [Manchester] United, Madrid, Barcelona or Milan, when the referees referee these kind of games, it's always difficult to go against these kind of teams. It's something the teams who are used to winning get all the time. We need to win games so we have this advantage in the future.

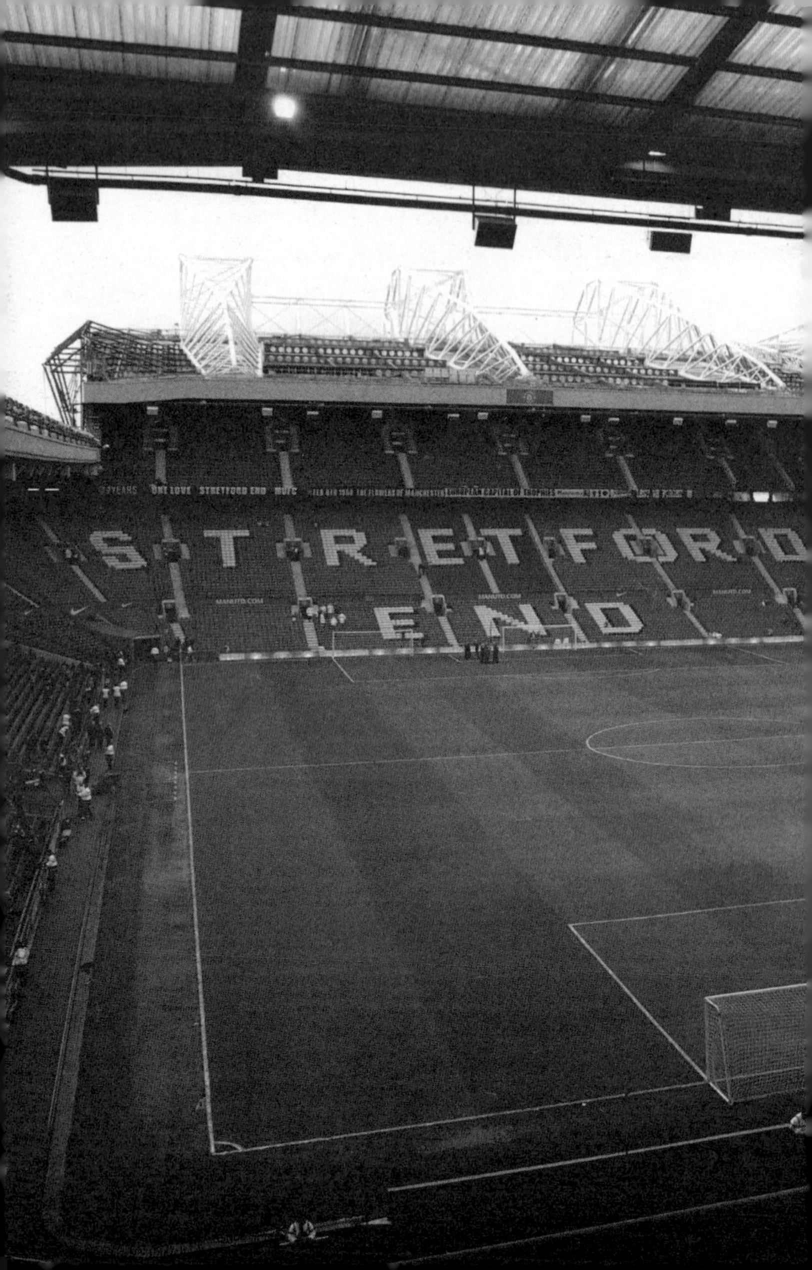
STRETFORD
END

The drama and heartbreak experienced by AC Milan, the perceived result of a couple of poor decisions over a 38-game season, could be dismissed as a disappointing one-off. When a refereeing anomaly affects the outcome of a decade's worth of fixtures as it evidently did for Manchester United it suggests that, at the very least, referees need help. The difficulty is determining exactly what to do about it. Goal-line technology may combat one element of the trend. It will remove even the most hostile and intimidating atmospheres from the equation and allow the referee to receive video assistance to achieve a calm, measured and hopefully accurate decision. However, it is at this point that Michel Platini would be most likely to interject. While most games will have their refereeing talking points, not every game will see a goal ruled out. Fewer still will see a goal ruled out because of a dispute over whether or not it has crossed the line. As Platini suggested, goal-line technology will merely scratch the surface of the discrepancies in football refereeing. The clamour for technology will only increase once fans see this element of the game better marshalled.

The real issue is that football is just too big a sport to perfect. There are too many debatable issues. Many are judgement calls – subjective and objective onlookers alike will always be divided. Emotive terms like 'deliberate handball' and 'tackling with intent' make the game impossible to control completely. But that's why so many love it. The injustices form part of a team's identity. Fans will bond over times they were 'cheated', over how they never get the rub of the green. There is even a sense of tribal belonging brought on by uniting to roar out defamatory chants about the referee. The debate, the drama, it is all part of football. Prior to the Premier League's decision to embrace technology, FIFA trialled a number of new schemes to improve refereeing decisions. Among these was the much-criticised addition of extra officials beside the goal, a measure made curious by the fact that these officials have rarely been seen to have involvement, noteworthy or otherwise. The truth is that technology would provide the best methods of clearing up those tough decisions, essentially enabling referees to rewind for a second look in the same way that pundits and commentators have for so many years. The referee's ability is limited; but when the alternative is a game punctuated by referral to devices and videos, it may be wiser to accept those limitations and keep football raw. Sepp Blatter's flippancy belies a truly salient point:

> I would say we shall live with the errors, not only the errors of the players and the coaches but we shall also live with the errors of the referees. So, let the game be as it is.

Jerome Boateng

Chapter 3

Imagine that ...

Footballers represent their place of birth ... and Africa surpasses its former colonisers

18 June 2010, 8.30pm. Cape Town Stadium, South Africa. The national football team of Algeria took to the pitch to face England in their second group game of the 2010 World Cup. As the teams lined up side by side, awaiting their respective national anthems, Rafik Halliche stood out for a surprising reason. The young Algeria-born defender was notable for exactly that – being born in Algeria. The rest of the starting eleven hailed from the land of their former colonisers, France. In a squad of 23, a staggering seventeen were French-born. Indeed, of all the nations competing at the 2010 World Cup, only seven out of 32 squads did NOT include foreign-born players: Argentina, Brazil, England, Honduras, Slovakia, Spain and Uruguay.

Algeria fielding France's 'B team' was not even the most

bizarre tale of dual nationality at the tournament. This came five days later and 860 miles away, at Soccer City, Johannesburg. In a match between Ghana and Germany two brothers, Jerome and Kevin-Prince Boateng, lined up on opposing sides. Both were born in Germany but, with a Ghanaian father, found themselves eligible to play for either nation. While both had represented Germany at youth level, Jerome chose to continue that affiliation while Kevin-Prince opted instead for Ghana. By the time kick-off came around the pair were no longer on speaking terms, their opposing allegiances leading to a bitter fall-out.

It's fair to say that, despite Germany winning that night, neither of the Boateng brothers regretted their choice. Jerome went on to win the third place play-off with Germany, while Kevin-Prince's goal against the USA helped Ghana on their way to becoming only the third African team ever to reach a World Cup quarter-final. Nevertheless, their match-up highlighted the messy and questionable nature of international selection.

There are a number of factors that have led to this situation and to truly understand the reasoning, you have to first understand the rules. FIFA make regular revisions of and amendments to their rulebook but the most up-to-date criteria for international selection as at the end of 2012 outlines four key scenarios. The first two are the most logical – that the player OR his biological parents were born within the borders of the relevant Football Association. So far, so simple, but the next two criteria have led to controversy. If a player's grandparents were born on the relevant territory

OR if the player has lived on the territory for at least two years then they also become eligible to represent the Association. National identity is a highly subjective matter, so arguably this is all well and good. Indeed, it is highly understandable that after two years of residence a player might feel significantly attached to a nation. But many would say that this is not enough.

So, when does a sense of dual nationality becomes unpatriotic opportunism? With football now very much a game driven by money and with the clubs paying the wages, it is perhaps inevitable that players will feel a greater sense of 'loyalty' to their club side than their country. One of the only clear advantages to a player of international over club football is the offer of a global stage. Only the elite European clubs can truly boast a guaranteed world presence in the form of the annual Champions League, a competition contested by the top sides from each European league and which in 2012 attracted over 150 million viewers worldwide for the final alone. As a result, numerous players and managers have spent many an hour studying family trees in the finest of detail in the hope of unearthing an ancestor from a nation with World Cup aspirations.

With the 2006 World Cup in Germany looming large, Trinidad and Tobago's squad was looking thin. They lacked quality in midfield, someone who could work them out of a tight spot against their technically superior group rivals, England, Sweden and Paraguay. A picturesque archipelago in the Gulf of Paria, the combined population of Trinidad and Tobago stood at only just over 1 million in 2006. To combat their lack of numbers in midfield, they drafted in Chris Birchall, who was playing in the third tier of English football for League One outfit Port Vale at the time. Birchall was not the only player from the lower reaches of the English league to feature in the World Cup; in fact he was joined by no fewer than seven other English-based players in the Trinidad and Tobago squad. These other inclusions attracted little more than local acclaim from their clubs and surrounding area, but Birchall made the national press. Why? He stood out somewhat among his teammates due to his distinctly European complexion and his broad Staffordshire accent. It was certainly an eye-catching choice, but since his mother had been born in Trinidad and Tobago it was, on paper at least, one of the less remarkable changes of allegiance in recent years. Nonetheless, Birchall's call-up once again got tongues wagging and journalists writing about the contentious topic of international selection.

The English FA are no strangers to skewing the line of descent either. In 2008, two years after Sven-Goran Eriksson was dismissed as England boss, the former FA chief executive released a book in which he outlined a number of Eriksson's plans for the team. In *FA Confidential* David Davies revealed that Eriksson had asked him to enquire about the availability of Italian-born goalkeeper Carlo Cudicini (pictured right) at the height of England's goalkeeping shortage. Cudicini had spent a number of years in the country playing for Chelsea and, having never represented Italy at senior level, was believed to be a possible candidate for an England call-up. Speculation of these discussions had

been rife at the time but, since Cudicini never joined up with the England squad, many dismissed it as tabloid fiction. He was not Sven's only foreign target either, as Davies divulged:

'Can you also find out about Malbranque, Edu and Saha?' Sven asked me. I wasn't sure what the public reaction would be to an Italian, a Brazilian and two Frenchmen coming into the squad but I did Sven's bidding.

None of Eriksson's foreign targets went on to play for England, and the overwhelming opinion of both fans and journalists on his tentative approaches was that such call-ups would cheapen international caps and destroy the morale of English-born hopefuls. The Swedish boss had long been pilloried in England for a perceived lack of appreciation of the traditions of English football, and news of Davies' foreign assignment only reinforced this reputation. Shortly after Sven's plans were formed – as so often happens when such speculation abounds – Saha and Edu received call-ups for their respective homelands, rendering them ineligible to represent England.

With international football drifting away from the patriotic calling it once was, fans and players in many parts of the world have come to see it as club football's support act – an intriguing but passionless version of the domestic game. But could this change have been averted if the rules on international call-ups had been stricter from the beginning?

Part of the reason why the criteria for call-ups have not been tightened is that any change would alter the pool of footballers for every country, effectively redrawing geographical borders. The increase in migration in recent decades has naturally led to a rise in dual nationality and citizenship. Of course, this is a wholly positive sign in terms of global harmony, but it has presented quite a quandary to the world of football. To draw the line one step further up or down the family tree would make a huge change to the international game.

If, for example, call-ups had been judged solely upon place of birth there might have been a power shift in the last half-century of international football. Some of the greatest teams in recent history have been built upon a foreign-born foundation. The France side that won the 1998 World Cup and then, with largely the same squad, went on to claim the 2000 European Championships featured a large and prominent foreign-born contingent. Many of their star names hailed from overseas; Marcel Desailly (Ghana), Patrick Vieira (Senegal), Lilian Thuram (Guadeloupe) and Christian Karembeu (New Caledonia).

Although many of these players hailed from nations under French political stewardship, all apart from New Caledonia had their own FIFA-recognised national teams. Removing these players from the French squad would have dealt a severe blow to their chances in both of the competitions in which they claimed victory, but the effect on the 'home' teams of these stars would have been far greater. Individually they might not have brought success to their nations, but having such big names as ambassadors might well have pushed them closer. (Ironically, the player widely regarded as the star of that French side, Zinedine Zidane, would under the existing rules have been eligible to play for Algeria should he have chosen to as both his parents were born there, though Zinedine was born in Marseille.)

Christian Karembeu

European and South American teams have dominated the world scene since football began, with no team from outside these two continents ever having won a World Cup. Edson Arantes do Nascimento, the Brazilian footballing genius better known as Pelé, was once famously quoted declaring that an African team would win the World Cup before the year 2000. It is a prediction that he has since denied making but, whether or not he said it, it did not come true. Pelé shed more light on the subject when explaining this misunderstanding to football magazine *FourFourTwo*. In addition to insisting that he had only ever said an African side *could*, rather than *would*, win a World Cup, Pelé outlined his reasoning behind this belief:

> I said that Africa produced a lot of good players and that as they went to Europe and learned more, they would get stronger. [...] In Africa, the domestic leagues are not strong and they are not organised, but the teams are always good.

This is the key. Europe is seen as the pinnacle of club football. Historically the top divisions in England, Spain and Italy have been considered the finest, with the Dutch, French and German leagues also featuring a very high standard of play. As a result players have flocked from across the globe to compete in these leagues, wanting to test themselves against the best. Pelé saw this as a good thing, but it has arguably been the downfall of African football. As Pelé identified, club competitions in Africa 'are not strong and they are not organised'. How can they be if the star players all flee to Europe at the first opportunity?

International success is an essential ingredient for domestic success as a nation's footballing pedigree grows over time. Alex Bellos, the former South America correspondent for the *Guardian* and author of *Futebol: The Brazilian Way of Life*, discovered just how true this is. In his book, Bellos spoke to a Brazilian football agent called Fábio who had the following to say:

> It's easier to place a Brazilian footballer in a team than it is a footballer of any other nationality. There is a worldwide fad for Brazilians. It's sad to say but it is much easier selling, for example, a crap Brazilian than a brilliant Mexican.

This is what African football is lacking. The pedigree. It is no coincidence that Brazil just happens to have won the World Cup more times than any other nation, or that due to a recent economic resurgence the domestic league has gone from strength to strength. While African individuals may flourish abroad, the lack of demand means that when they come to be sold the fees are relatively meagre. This in turn depletes the domestic leagues without putting anything back in, so the clubs cannot afford to replace the players or to invest in coaching or facilities to foster new talent.

There is the odd exception to this rule, such as Ajax Cape Town, a South African branch of the famous Dutch club, which coaches local players with a view to exporting them to

the Netherlands. However, the result is ultimately the same; the best talent is plucked out rather than remaining to raise the profile of the league.

This may all sound like a world away from Marcel Desailly and Patrick Vieira choosing France over their respective nations of birth, but it is all connected. Should Desailly have chosen to represent Ghana, it would have been a single step towards redressing the balance in football worldwide; so too for Vieira and Senegal. The choice was theirs, they opted against it and it is hard to blame them.

There are countless stories of African players perishing while attempting to cross frontiers and borders to escape peril at home and reach the footballing havens of southern and western Europe; less well known are the equally dramatic tales of players struggling to gain a return to their homelands.

In 1958, a sensational story unfurled involving a group of Algerian nationals based in France. At the time Algeria and France had been at war for four years, a war waged by Algeria in an attempt to gain independence. With the World Cup in Sweden two months away, nationalist feelings were running high. The tub-thumping of the French was backed up by a very talented squad. Much like the team that triumphed in 1998 and 2000, it was not a purely 'French' squad. There was a strong smattering of Algerian talent throughout the team, including Moustapha Zitouni and Rachid Mekhloufi, two of the region's stars.

On 15 April 1958, ten of *Les Bleus'* Algerian players defected, setting off for the Tunisian capital Tunis under cover of darkness. There they joined a political movement known as the Front de Libération Nationale (FLN) who had masterminded the exodus. It was a small but powerful protest against the ruling nation. Over the following months the FLN side pitted their skills against any team who would go up against them. They struggled to find willing opposition as their existence contravened FIFA rules; however, they remained unbeaten in their first seven matches, including an impressive 6–1 victory over Yugoslavia and a 7–0 rout of Libya. More telling was the void they left in the French squad, who had travelled to Sweden for the World Cup as planned. They still managed to put on a strong show, breezing past the quarter-final stage of the tournament with Morocco-born striker Just Fontaine notching up an outstanding thirteen goals. It was in the semi-finals that the missing Algerian contingent were most missed. Having faced competitive but not altogether formidable opposition in the lead-up (Yugoslavia, Scotland, Paraguay and Wales), they met Brazil in the semi-final. France lost out in a 5–2 defeat. It was a golden era for France, and many still maintain that with the Algerian players the outcome would have been different. The incident highlights the vital role African-born players have played for other nations and just how damaging their absence could and would be if the rules were changed. After all, even without the Algerians, France's leading marksman was still not French-born.

It is astounding to see just how many of the world's most prestigious footballing nations are built on a foreign foundation. Portugal's Eusebio was born in Mozambique. Many

Eusebio

of the Netherlands greats hail from the South American former Dutch colony of Surinam, including Edgar Davids, Clarence Seedorf and Jimmy Floyd Hasselbaink. In 2006 Simone Perrotta became the first English-born player for 40 years to lift a World Cup, having spent his first four years in England before relocating to Italy.

The footballing landscape would look completely different today if international call-ups had been restricted to a player's birthplace. The likes of France, Germany and Portugal would have been weakened considerably while the likes of Morocco, Algeria, Poland and many other traditionally unfancied sides would have prospered. The change would have prevented Algeria fielding a nearly all-French lineup in 2010, but with a different footballing history they might not have had to. The African triumph that Pelé may or may not have predicted could so easily have come to pass, be it Eusebio's Mozambique, Just Fontaine's Morocco or some other 'European' icon leading his native land to glory. Most importantly of all, the African domestic leagues could be thriving, with Europe's greatest stars looking to ply their trade on African soil.

Chapter 4

Imagine that ...

Zaire concedes after comical free-kick against Brazil ... and African football regresses for years to come

Football, at its core, is a very simple game. Two sides, eleven men against eleven, trying to put one ball into two goals over 90 minutes. Add formations, tactics and weather conditions

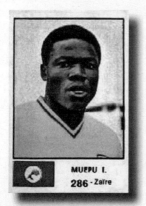

MUEPU I.
286 - Zaïre

to the mix and you have the building blocks of the world's most popular sport. Outside forces sometimes complicate the game, usually to its detriment. In recent years money has caused problems in football, through financial mismanagement and betting scandals. However, in 1974 Zaire international Joseph Mwepu Ilunga and his teammates were confronted by factors far more

serious than any of these. The result was one of the most bizarre and misunderstood incidents in World Cup history.

The 1974 World Cup was held in West Germany. It was a tournament of firsts. It was the first and last international tournament to feature West and East Germany as separate sides. It was the first time that the modern-day World Cup trophy was used, the Brazilians holding on to the previous Jules Rimet trophy following an unprecedented three World Cup victories. Most striking of all was the presence of Zaire (now the Democratic Republic of Congo) who became the first black African side to ever qualify for the World Cup finals. It was a momentous occasion for the continent as a whole; a chance to test their mettle in front of the watching world – and a test is exactly what they got. Drawn in a qualifying group against the formidable Brazilians, a robust Yugoslavia and a Scotland team boasting such talents as Billy Bremner, Kenny Dalglish and Jimmy 'Jinky' Johnstone, Zaire would have to exceed all expectations to even compete in their group.

Zaire's president, Mobutu Sésé Seko (pictured left), took a close interest in the football team; after all, they were set to gain greater exposure for the nation than it had ever had before. He did his best to mould the team in his own image. After coming to power, Mobutu replaced their former nickname, the 'Lions', with the more flamboyant leopard.

In an interview with *Shoot!* magazine in the lead-up to West Germany '74, Zaire's captain Mantantu Kidumu spoke about President Mobutu's reaction when they qualified for the tournament:

President Mobutu presented each one of us with a house made of brick, a new car and a holiday for us and our families to the United States. I don't know what he plans to give us if we win the World Cup!

It was, however, defeat that would hold the biggest shock for Kidumu and his teammates.

The first game was against the Scots and provided no shocks. In an underwhelming but respectable start, Zaire fell in a 2–0 defeat. Played out in front of Borussia Dortmund's half-full Westfalenstadion, the match revealed a noticeable lack of maturity in the Zaire squad. Scotland had made the most of their opponents' naivety with goals from Peter Lorimer and Joe Jordan, but the Leopards had not disgraced themselves. A tougher test was to follow four days later in Gelsenkirchen, in the form of Yugoslavia. Fresh off the back of a morale-boosting 0–0 draw with reigning champions Brazil, the Yugoslavs smelled blood. The predatory instincts of

the so-called Leopards were not in evidence as Yugoslavia struck goal after goal after goal. Five separate scorers had breached the Zairian defence by half-time and the game finished 9–0. Zaire, and more troublingly President Mobutu, were left humiliated.

With a game against Brazil looming, the nation feared further embarrassment. President Mobutu acted swiftly to make clear that this was not an option. A public announcement was put out across Zairian radio and television, summoning the squad to a meeting with the president. Whatever Mobutu had to say, the public

nature of the summoning ensured that the team were left in no doubt as to the importance of their performance in the following fixture.

The day of the game soon arrived and the squad returned to the scene of their nine-goal hammering, the Parkstadion in Gelsenkirchen. 36,000 fans had congregated in the stands to see a unique battle of styles; the masters of the game against comparative novices. The Zairian defence managed to hold strong for four minutes longer than they had in their previous fixture, with the formidable Jairzinho striking after twelve minutes. The Leopards were set firmly in damage-limitation mode with nearly 80 minutes of the game remaining. Remarkably, against all of the attacking flair and penetration of the Brazilians, at half-time the score was still 1–0. The second half saw an equally robust performance from the Africans; it took the Brazilians a

further twenty minutes after the break to breach their defence, before doing so again in the 79th minute. As the game headed into the closing stages it appeared that Zaire, although set to exit the competition, were going to leave

with their heads held high. 3–0 against Brazil was a respectable score-line by almost anyone's reckoning, and were it not for Mobutu's demands then Zaire would most likely have been content with their showing.

The match seemed to be petering out. Then, five minutes from time, Brazil were awarded a free-kick five yards outside the Zaire box. Jairzinho and Rivelinho, two masters of free-kick taking, stood over the ball. The three-goal margin looked under threat.

As the Brazilians stood, pondering their approach, a lone figure broke free from the Zaire defensive wall. When Mwepu Ilunga reached the motionless ball he propelled it back down the pitch, towards the Brazilian goal. Everyone else watched incredulously, the referee immediately brandishing a yellow card. John Motson, commentating for the BBC at the time, declared it to be 'a bizarre moment of African ignorance'. Many were unsure quite what they had just seen. It resembled the petulance of a schoolyard

football match, but there had not been anything particularly contentious about the decision to award a free-kick.
Mwepu Ilunga's clearance appeared to be fuelled by blind
panic, not any burning sense of injustice. Nevertheless,
after a moment's head-scratching and guffawing, the free-
kick was eventually retaken and successfully defended. The
game finished 3–0, but Zaire's pride was somewhat dented
by the bizarre actions of Mwepu Ilunga and confusion over
his thought process continued long after the game's end.

Their World Cup campaign had begun in such promising fashion, drawing begrudging praise from Scotland
manager Willie Ormond in the process. Ormond had
said: 'Zaire were an eye-opener. Their control is on the
ground, with the accent always on attack, as fresh as a summer breeze on a lovely summer night.' By the time their
involvement in the competition ended they were receiving
no such praise; they had become the punchline of the
world's jokes.

However, Zaire were not new to the game. They were
the reigning African champions, having won the African
Nations Cup in March of the same year. While this was not
a tournament on the same level as the World Cup, it was a
FIFA-accredited competition contested by the best teams
of an entire continent. It was simply inconceivable that
what Ilunga had done was the result of cultural differences
and a different take on the rules. As Mwepu Ilunga later
revealed, President Mobutu had said that the performance
of the team and him in particular had 'set back the percep-
tion of African football twenty years'. Surely there had to

be more to the story than, as John Motson had so bluntly put it, African ignorance.

The scathing assessment from Mobutu was typical of the man. Rising to power on the back of a series of military coups during the 1960s Congo crisis, Mobutu was a daunting individual. Having spent his youth in the Zairian army before taking the role of army chief of staff, he later went on to overthrow the very man who had granted him the position, President Lumumba. When Mobutu found himself the target of a military coup, thirteen years on, he instructed his troops to shoot on sight as he successfully suppressed the onslaught. His reputation throughout Zaire was fearsome. When it was announced that he had summoned the national football team following the defeat to the Yugoslavs, few envied the players.

Years after the 1974 World Cup, the man whom Mobutu had singled out for the most damning criticism gave his side of the story. Ilunga first explained that the Brazil game was not the start of the trouble between Mobutu and the national team. Mobutu was keen to ensure that Zaire would come to be associated with sporting prowess and made a habit of throwing vast sums of money at this aim. Shortly before the 1974 World Cup he laid out the grand sum of $5 million to boxing promoter Don King for Zaire to host a heavyweight boxing match between Muhammad Ali and George Fore-

ZAÏRE 74

ALI et FOREMAN FONT CONFIANCE A MOBUTU

VOUS AUSSI FAITES COMME EUX , AYEZ

CONFIANCE EN MOBUTU

man. The fight went on to be dubbed the 'Rumble in the Jungle' and is one of the most famous bouts in history.

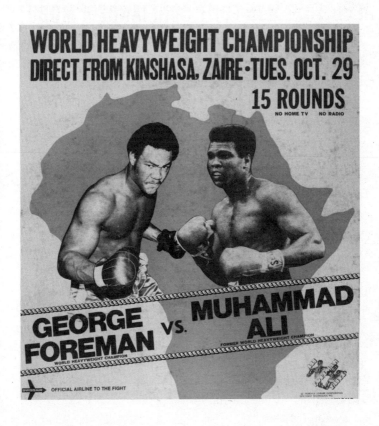

Mobutu offered similar riches to the Zaire football team should they perform admirably in West Germany but, on the eve of the Yugoslavia match, the players received new information. Ilunga explained: 'Before the Yugoslavia match we learnt that we were not going to be paid, so we refused to play.' Of course they did play, but their standard reflected the distraction of players who had been coerced into turning up against their will.

It might seem disappointing that the players could be so unpatriotic as to require financial persuasion to represent their nation, but the pre-Yugoslavia U-turn from Mobutu was just a glimpse of a far graver situation for the Zairian players. Unlike many of the other teams competing at the World Cup, Zaire's squad consisted solely of amateurs. This was not by chance. As the inevitable 9–0 drubbing played out and Mobutu's ire grew greater, he planned his fateful meeting with the team. It was another of the Leopards, striker Adelard Mayanga, who later divulged one of Mobutu's more unsettling outbursts from that meeting: 'I can tell you all now that you are not going to be like the Senegalese, the Ivorians, the Cameroonians who go and play overseas.' Mobutu promptly banned any players from exiting the Zairian leagues to play elsewhere. This had been an unwritten rule throughout Mobutu's time in office, but he left the players in no doubt that the ban stood firm. Since the Zairian leagues were not professional, the transfer ban effectively imposed a ceiling on the players. What's more, without their international bonuses their futures looked increasingly bleak.

Mobutu's threats extended beyond forced residence: 'After the match, he sent his presidential guards to threaten us,' said Ilunga in a 2002 interview with the BBC. 'They closed the hotel to all journalists and said that if we lost 0–4 to

Brazil, none of us would be able to return home.' Suddenly Ilunga's 'comical' free-kick clearance starts to make sense. Far from the African ignorance that Motson had believed he was observing, Ilunga understood the situation all too well. 'Most of the Brazil players, and the crowd too, thought it was hilarious. I shouted, "You b*stards!" at them because they didn't understand the pressure we were under.' As we know, Zaire managed to avoid the perilous 0–4 scoreline, but the football of sub-Saharan Africa might have been damaged unalterably had the boys from Brazil managed to strike just once more.

Over the course of the following decade or so, there was a power shift in African football. Zaire's World Cup debut had whetted the appetite and raised the expectations of the whole of sub-Saharan Africa. Whereas the Arabic nations, such as Egypt, Algeria and Tunisia, had dominated the African Cup of Nations and by extension World Cup qualifying for decades, by the time the 1990 World Cup in Italy came around, the southern nations were ready to try again. With the qualifying stages in Africa changing from a knockout system to a league for the first time, the Cameroonians were able to overcome the traditional dominance of Tunisia, Egypt and Morocco to qualify. The minimal TV exposure of African football meant that their opposition had little idea of whom or what they were set to face. As such, Cameroon's team was the surprise package at the tournament, much as Zaire had been in '74. Even more surprisingly, their stand-out performer was a 38-year-old striker who had only recently left the spotlight of the French leagues to compete on the

remote French island of Réunion. Roger Milla took the tournament by storm, helping Cameroon out with four priceless goals as the nation reached the quarter-finals. His image was made famous by his trademark goal celebration, running off to the corner flag before performing an exotic dance with it. Their exit eventually came when they were knocked out by clear favourites England, but they managed to hold a 2–1 lead until the final minutes before conceding again in extra time. It was a valiant effort from the Indomitable Lions.

Once Cameroon had shown that a nation from the region was capable of competing against the best teams in the world, African sides became a regular fixture in later World Cups. In 1994 they returned, joined this time by Nigeria. While Cameroon failed to make it out of the group stages, Nigeria continued in similar fashion to the Cameroonians' 1990 campaign. They reached the knockout stages before being sent home in extra time at the hands of prestigious opposition. It wasn't England that broke African hearts this time around, but Italy. Four years later in France, three sub-Saharan teams qualified; Cameroon and Nigeria retained their places and South Africa joined them.

The trend continued until eventually FIFA sat up and took notice. In 2004, the right to host the 2010 World Cup was awarded to South Africa. With the hosts granted automatic qualification, the region was given an extra place in the finals. An unprecedented six African sides competed in the tournament, five of which were from south of the Sahara. The region's fortunes in the competition were mixed, with Cameroon and Nigeria failing to impress, while South

Africa, Algeria and the Ivory Coast battled bravely but without joy in difficult groups. Ghana, however, repeated the feat of Cameroon in 1990 as they became only the second African nation ever to reach the quarter-finals. They would have progressed further were it not for a handball from Uruguay's Luis Suarez stopping the ball on the line. Ghana missed the resulting penalty and crashed out following a dramatic shoot-out. Regardless of the disappointing end to their involvement in the competition, it was a watershed moment in African and world football alike. From the novelty of Zaire's calamitous showing in 1974 to a commanding and impressive presence in 2010, in just under 25 years the transformation of the continent's footballing pedigree was quite sensational.

All of this progress would not have been possible if Brazil had managed to score a fourth goal in 1974 and Mobutu had acted upon his threats. FIFA have an admirable history of banning nations from competing over racial or civil rights issues. One of Africa's strongest sporting nations experienced this first-hand between 1958 and 1992 as South Africa were banned because of the apartheid regime. Should Mobutu have carried out his threats to the players, there is little doubt that Zaire would have been removed from any further competitions. As it happens, Zaire's appearance in 1974 is their only World Cup appearance to date, but their exploits at that tournament kick-started a legacy for their continent, if not their country. Should Zaire have joined South Africa on FIFA's blacklist, the reputation of the entire region would have been sullied. With a further competitor removed from its numbers, the African Cup of Nations would have undoubtedly suffered too.

Mwepu Ilunga sadly passed away in 1998 after sustaining a fatal gunshot wound. He had seen out his final years in a penniless state, seemingly a forgotten man. His former teammate Ndaye Mulamba later paid a bittersweet tribute: 'In Europe they honour their footballers. Here, when you play they know you but when you finish they forget you.' His words made for painful reading and highlighted the tragic demise of a true icon. Mwepu Ilunga must never be forgotten, for without his brave efforts the world of football would be a very different place.

Chapter 5

Imagine that ...

Football moves to soften its image midway through the 20th century ... and a nation's footballing identity is transformed

Football has cleaned up its image in recent years, but as the cleansing continues, so too do the calls for a return to the 'good old days'. A romanticised nostalgia is only natural but it goes beyond that; football today is completely different to the game that was played no more than 20 or 30 years ago. Many of football's most famous moments might never have occurred had modern-day rules been in place.

The protective element of the new laws can be seen in almost any game on any continent. Gone are the bone-crunching tackles from behind, and with them the accompanying piles of crumpled players. In their place are 'soft bookings' and players 'simulating', or diving. These oft-maligned side-effects have led to regular claims that football is becoming a non-contact sport. This is, it appears, an unavoidable trade-off.

When Argentine prodigy Lionel Messi broke onto the scene he was the latest in a long line of players dubbed 'the new Maradona'. It had long been an affliction which burdened Argentina's young talents and, while many had gone on to forge admirable careers, none had quite managed to reach the heights of Maradona at his peak. However, Messi was not just another also-ran. In 2007 his Barcelona side took to the pitch to face Getafe in the semi-final of the Spanish Cup, otherwise known as the Copa del Rey. In the 29th minute, with Barcelona already a goal up, the diminutive Argentine took possession of the ball just within his own half, wide out on the right wing. His first task was to evade the oncoming challenges of two Getafe players. He did so

Lionel Messi

with ease. Then, from a seemingly innocuous position, he began to drive forward, skipping past the flailing legs of the opposition. Ten seconds later he was running towards his adoring fans to celebrate a magnificent solo effort.

If the jinking brilliance of the goal was not enough to convince people that Messi was at least a contender for Maradona's mantle, then the accompanying sense of déjà vu surely was. It was a carbon copy of the goal Maradona had scored against England in the 1986 World Cup two decades earlier, a goal that had been nicknamed 'Goal of the Century', an unofficial but rarely disputed accolade. He had started in the same part of the field, followed the same meandering path, and rounded the goalkeeper in exactly the same manner. A relic had been revived, yet still some remained unconvinced. The battering that Maradona had evaded on the way was the difference, they argued. While Messi passed players who were vying for the ball, Maradona's opponents aimed for ankles, shins, legs. This does not make Messi's feat less remarkable.

This is only one side of the argument. Where does this leave the defenders? Should the achievements of those from bygone eras be devalued because the tackling was more robust then? Among the defenders that Maradona hurdled en route to scoring his wonder goal was one Terry Butcher. Another much-loved face of 1980s football, the devoted following amassed by Butcher throughout a career in the English and Scottish leagues was somewhat different to that of Maradona. Butcher's tough tackling appealed to a British sense of battle. Maradona's weaving runs provided the flair

and expression that the Argentinians craved. A culture clash perhaps, but it highlights the tricky business of regulating a game with a global reach.

Terry Butcher's most iconic moment is another reminder of football's past. In September 1989, England travelled to Stockholm to face Sweden. There was a lot at stake: England needed to come away from the Swedish capital with at least a draw or else they would fail to qualify for the 1990 World Cup in Italy. Just minutes into the match their hopes were dealt a colossal blow. An essential brick in their defensive wall, team captain Terry Butcher leapt high above two Swedish midfielders to head a stray ball clear, but in doing so clashed heads with his challenger. The pair fell to the ground before groggily returning to their feet. Blood was streaming from Butcher's head. Undeterred, he waited

while the team doctor applied stitches and bandages before returning to the action. Far from being cautious from then on, Butcher proceeded to challenge for each and every aerial ball and before long was covered in his own blood. So too was the ball, and the opposition for that matter. Every header sent blood splattering. England went on to clinch the point they so desperately needed, in no small part due to Butcher's defensive efforts. The post-match photographs of him standing with his white shirt and bandages drenched in his blood have long since been held up as a snapshot of an English bulldog spirit.

Today, however, the iconic image of Terry Butcher would never have appeared. He would have been forced to replace his bloodied shirt and shorts with clean replicas once blood started to spill. There is, of course, clear reasoning behind this change. In 2004 the *British Journal of Sports Medicine* conducted a review of sporting practices relating to blood-borne infections. The report's findings were numerous and wide-reaching, as it was a multi-purpose review designed to inform sport in its entirety and not just football. Among other advice, its main conclusion was that a preventative approach needed to be taken:

> Any equipment contaminated with blood should be removed from the sports activity area; if this is not pos-sible – for example, a wrestling mat – the item must be cleaned and dried appropriately (using disposable cloths and a fresh solution of one part household bleach to ten parts water).

Terry Butcher

With Hepatitis B and C and HIV all transmissible by blood it made perfect sense. The inconvenience of having to change out of bloodied garments, whether that was a red speck or a Butcher-esque soaking, paled in comparison to the threat of serious infection. It was a necessary clean-up, but one that spelled the end of a 'blood, sweat and tears' era.

Butcher's finest moment is not the only iconic feat of endurance that would have been erased by stricter health and safety rulings. In 1966, following a nineteen-day tournament that had seen him feature in five games and 120 minutes of a World Cup final against West Germany, England striker Geoff Hurst found himself rushing towards goal with the ball at his feet. Kenneth Wolstenholme was commentating for the BBC. 'Some people are on the pitch. They think it's all over. It is now,' he exclaimed, as Hurst thumped the ball beyond the goalkeeper. It was a moment of pure serendipity. The fans celebrating before the goal had even been scored, the tantalising unfurling of Wolstenholme's words, the crowning moment of host nation England's victorious World Cup campaign. Today, however, Wolstenholme's momentous commentary would have been cut short. The pitch invasion he had described, the 'people on the pitch', would have led play being stopped and Hurst being robbed of his cup final hat-trick.

So would it really have mattered if Hurst's hat-trick strike had been ruled out due to pitch invasion, or if Butcher had played on in a clean shirt? The eventual outcomes are unlikely to have differed greatly. If only it were that simple. The wholesale improvements to health and safety in football have been the result of many factors, and have gone hand in hand with a faster-paced game.

Naturally, the regulations shape the players and in turn the style of play. One example of this is a change in the rules on treating injuries that has had a marked effect on tactical gamesmanship in football. Up until 2006 injuries during play were covered by a long-standing 'gentleman's agreement': if a player remained on the floor following a collision, it was commonplace for the opposition to put the ball out of play so as not to take advantage of their extra man. The inherent flaw in this agreement is that it relies on honesty and goodwill, which is often missing, especially in the latter stages of important games. This convention was often invoked in an unsportsmanlike way to prevent promising counterattacks, with players squirming dramatically until play stopped. Although the rule was unwritten, it was so entrenched that booing and whistling from the crowd usually led to the attacking side being pressured into relenting. It was an admirable convention but as a 'win at all costs' mentality crept into the sport, it became arcane and unsavoury. The tipping point came in the 2006 World Cup in Germany as games were constantly halted by exaggerated injury, and a decision was taken to hand the responsibility of stopping play over to the referee. In 2012 Arsenal manager Arsène Wenger gave his views on the transition, claiming players 'are scared of being unpopular or criticised by the media if they don't do it'. The solution is a work in progress, but something clearly had to change.

Another aspect of football that needed cleaning up was the way in which outfield players were allowed to challenge goalkeepers. For decades a loose ball in the penalty area was the prelude to bloodshed. Fans were used to seeing goalkeeper and attacker alike grit their teeth and wince before throwing themselves studs first or headlong towards the

ball. Goalkeepers were commonly clattered and shoved over the line and the goal would stand.

Goalkeepers were made of sterner stuff in those days. During the Second World War a German paratrooper was captured by the English and kept as a prisoner of war. He took to playing in goal during football matches within the camp, and by the time the war ended he was good enough to play professionally. He signed first for St Helens Town before later securing a contract at Manchester City, the club where he would go on to make his name. That name was Bert Trautmann. He has come to be associated with endurance and perseverance following his exceptional involvement in the 1956 FA Cup final against Birmingham City. With seventeen minutes remaining and with City 3–1 up,

Birmingham were on the attack. As striker Peter Murphy bore down on goal looking certain to score, Trautmann came hurtling out, throwing himself at Murphy's feet. Murphy clattered into him but the brave keeper came away with the ball as City maintained their 3–1 lead. Trautmann lifted the cup and went home to nurse his wounds. It only emerged three days later that the German had broken his neck in the challenge before playing out the remaining seventeen minutes. Due to rule changes such a clash would probably not happen today, but in any case it is hard to think of any modern goalkeeper who would be robust enough to continue playing with such an injury.

Few people would want to return to the environment that brought about such a horrific injury, yet when it comes to outfield players feelings are more mixed, varying from country to country, culture to culture. Traditionally technical footballing nations such as Spain and Brazil prioritise thoughtfulness and creativity, with physical confrontation kept to a minimum. In Italy and Germany the thinking is that there is little need to foul if you can intercept. Defend-

ing is an art in these nations, something that has been both a contributor to and the result of defensive masters such as Franco Baresi and Franz Beckenbauer. British football is far more primal. Whereas other nations see unnecessary physicality in the sport as juvenile and uncultured, in Britain it is a traditional show of dominance. Many fans want to see routine displays of brute strength and ruthlessness in their outfield players, or at least those in defensive roles. Players shirking strong challenges in the British leagues are seen as uncommitted, whereas overseas they might be considered pragmatic and sensible in avoiding a possibly dangerous collision. Refereeing is paramount when teams differ in their approach to tackling. Too stern and the more physical team will be at a disadvantage; too lenient and the technical team will get brutalised.

With each alteration of the rulebook, the requirements for success change too. Teams at all levels will adapt to best embrace rule changes and enhance their chances of winning. It is no coincidence that in the years since the rules surrounding challenges on goalkeepers were tweaked, the techniques and habits of goalkeepers have changed too. Aside from no longer requiring the physical bulk and brawn that was once a staple of a keeper's makeup, it is often said that modern goalkeepers are incapable of holding on to a ball. Football's elder supporters reminisce about the glory days: 'In my day Gordon Banks would have held on to that ... and only using one hand!' It is a facet of the evolution of goalkeeping. Without the threat of a centre forward clattering into you every time the ball nears your hands, the skill of holding on to a ball becomes less essential. It has been replaced by shot-stopping, parrying and punching clear instead of trying to hold the ball and accidentally dropping it at the feet of a striker waiting to poach – the wiry poaching striker having outlasted the burly, brutish centre forward due to the same changes.

This instinctive adaptation means that the rules and regulations surrounding football will never stop at controlling the state of professional play. They will always reshape the game at the grass-roots level. In the same way that celebrity footballers are burdened with the tag of role models and vilified for diving or feigning injury, the rule makers and refereeing bodies need to take responsibility. They set the parameters of play and as such are just as influential in the prevalence of gamesmanship. Although an earlier change in the rules relating to blood injuries probably wouldn't have changed the outcome of Terry Butcher and England's match against Sweden, a history of stricter refereeing in Britain surely would have. Without such lenience on tough tackling and robust play it is highly unlikely that, with his natural attributes, Terry Butcher would have managed to gain such prominence in English football. He might have been replaced by an English equivalent of Franco Baresi or Franz Beckenbauer. And in turn, that change could have brought about a golden era of technical English attacking players, comfortable with the ball at their feet without the threat of defensive 'hard men' bearing down on them.

The world of football is a complex one, with no two elements completely separate. The nostalgic aura created by a childhood spent falling in love with the beautiful game makes it inevitable that fans will pine for football's 'good old days'. However, if those days were to return then the fast-paced, no-nonsense matches so many clamour for would more than likely be replaced by stop-start, injury-filled farces. Footballers are now a different breed entirely, and in such an environment the likes of Lionel Messi would not last long.

Chapter 6

Imagine that ...

Torino's greats survive beyond the 1940s ... and set the standard for football across the globe

The greatest players and teams in football gain immortal status. Johan Cruyff's free-moving 'Total Footballing' Netherlands side of the 1970s will forever be romanticised by fans of the game. The Hungary side which finished runners-up in the 1954 World Cup, the 'Magnificent Magyars' spearheaded by the inimitable Ferenc Puskás, are the stuff of legend. It's not a phenomenon specific to international sides. Still loved is the AC Milan team of the late 1980s, resplendent with the attacking bite of Marco van Basten and Ruud Gullit, backed up by the defensive steel of Paolo Maldini and Franco Baresi. More recently, the Barcelona side built around the otherworldly Lionel Messi has been mooted for footballing folklore. Some teams, however, are forgotten by all except those who witnessed their magic.

In the 1940s one team seemed destined to have secured the cooing admiration of journalists and supporters for years to come. Their greatness on the pitch broke records and decimated opposition defences. Yet today most people outside Italy would struggle to name a single member of their great side. They have drifted out of football's collective memory to be replaced by their rivals, including Turin neighbours Juventus. The team in question is Torino, *Il Grande Torino* – the Great Torino, or so they could have been. Considering how little is now known about this sensational team, their dominance was anything but fleeting.

There is no shortage of examples when it comes to encapsulating Torino's prowess. To this day they still hold records in the Italian game. They were showmen and still hold the record for most goals in a single Serie A season, scoring a stunning 125 goals in 40 games during the season of 1947/48. Their single greatest performance came two seasons earlier. On 28 April 1946 Torino travelled south to the Stadio Olimpico in Rome, home to Lazio and AS Roma. On this particular day it was Roma they were up against, but in next to no time the home side probably wished Lazio were in their place. Torino struck early and often. By the twenty-minute mark the score was starting to get embarrassing; Torino were six goals up. The rest of the game was an exhibition of superiority as Torino ruled over Roma, retaining possession impeccably. Manager Luigi Ferrero had given the word to his players to ease off on their hapless opponents. The job was already complete and they eased through the remaining 70 minutes, scoring just once more before exiting the pitch to rapturous applause and a standing ovation. More than half a century later it remains Roma's heaviest league defeat, although in 1947 Torino came close to lowering the bar further as they again scored seven after Roma had taken a 1–0 lead.

For such dominance it seems inconceivable that the legacy of such a side should be erased, but on 4 May 1949 that is what happened. *Il Grande Torino* were in much demand at the time; everyone wanted a chance to see the spectacle. On 1 May the team had travelled to Lisbon for a testimonial match in honour of Benfica captain Jose Ferreira. The Serie A season was still in progress but, following a vital 0–0 draw with rivals Inter Milan that left them

sitting four points clear with four games to go, Torino agreed to take a short break. The match against Benfica was a typically high-scoring affair with Torino graciously succumbing to the star of the show, losing 4–3 to Ferreira's Benfica. Tragedy struck when they came to return home, hoping to finish off the final leg of their season and claim an unprecedented fifth consecutive league trophy. Travelling by plane, the team had begun their approach into Turin when things started to go wrong. The pilot was Pierluigi Meroni, a greatly respected man and a decorated war veteran. Turin was obscured by cloud and the rain was lashing down. Conditions were treacherous. As the plane broke clear of the clouds Meroni became all too aware of their predicament. He had mistaken their positioning and they were hurtling towards Turin far lower than he had intended. The Superga hills surrounded them and sadly there was no way out. Meroni fought in vain to reroute the aircraft as *Il Torino Grande* crashed head-on into an exterior wall of the Basilica of Superga (pictured opposite), positioned at the peak of one of the hills. Flames and showering debris engulfed Superga. There were no survivors; all 31 passengers and crew members perished.

The mourning was heartfelt and widespread. A funeral was held two days later in Turin and thousands attended. It has been estimated that over half a million people lined the streets as the funeral cortège passed through, trailing behind a symbolically empty team bus – the *Conte Rosso* or Red Count. It was a tragedy that hit the entire nation, not least because of the commanding role that Torino's stars

had played in the Italian national team. They had regularly contributed over half of the Azzurri's players; in May 1947 Italy had beaten Hungary with a side that included only one non-Torino player, the Juventus goalkeeper Lucido Sentimenti. Many Italians still feel that, with the help of the fallen Torino team, Italy could have added to their impressive haul of four World Cups. They won consecutively in 1934 and '38, but no further tournament took place until 1950 due to the Second World War and its aftermath, so Italy were unable to use their wealth of Turin-based talent. This is a large factor in the relative anonymity of the illustrious Torino side, since they were never able to show off their talents on the global stage.

Following the Superga disaster Torino fielded youth players for the final four games of the season and managed to seal the trophy. The youngsters proudly upheld the standards of the club with a 4–0 victory against Genoa in the team's first game after the crash. The title slipped from their reach the following season, with city rivals Juventus prevailing as Torino slumped to sixth place. A mini-revival the following season saw them finish in second, but since then victory in 1975/76 remains their only further league win to date.

Although Torino excelled as a unit, they were just as impressive as individuals. Like most of the great teams in history, *Il*

Grande Torino had a magnificent jewel in their crown and his name was Valentino Mazzola (pictured above). Deployed as an attacking midfielder, Mazzola was central to everything Torino did. As good going forward as he was in defence, immaculate in the air or with the ball at his feet, he quite simply had it all. His peers regularly described him as the 'complete player' and he attracted praise from throughout the sport. Mazzola's teammate Mario Rigamonti once said: 'He alone is half the squad, the other half is made by the rest of us together.' Enzo Bearzot, the coach who finally led Italy to their third World Cup in 1982, is as qualified a voice as any when it comes to assessing Italian talents. He said: 'The greatest Italian player of all time was Valentino Mazzola; he was a man who could carry his whole team.'

It would be easy to assume that the source of Torino's success was ten great players led by one phenomenal talent, but Mazzola was not naïve enough to overlook the work of the team, realising that his colleagues enabled him to prosper. 'Football will always be a game of eleven,' Mazzola once said. This mantra was central to Torino's great achievements, as it was to many of the teams that followed in their footsteps. Before Torino, football had been far more compartmentalised. Centre halves prowled the field between the goalkeeper and the midfield but rarely strayed beyond. Strikers would hunt for space among the opposition's defenders and were not expected to abandon that role. What Torino pioneered was complete contribution. Players would help one another out regardless of their position. Victories like the two seven-goal routs against Roma were made possible by the sheer intensity of their play. Attacking as a unit, defending in numbers, Torino's games were regularly won in the first half, if not by the number of goals scored then by the exhausting tempo to which they subjected the opposition.

This may sound suspiciously similar to the famous Dutch export of Total Football, a system made famous by Johan Cruyff. However, there was a key difference. Total Football, or *totaalvoetbal* as the Dutch call it, was the result of meticulous planning and football theory. It came from the classroom. That's not to say that Torino's approach was not methodically thought out, just that it originated in a different place. Total Football was the brainchild of Dutch coach Rinus Michels, who had the following to say on his approach:

> It is an art in itself to compose a starting team, finding the balance between creative players and those with destructive powers, and between defence, construction and attack – never forgetting the quality of the opposition and the specific pressures of each match.

The results may have been very similar, but the methodology was vastly different. Torino's approach stemmed from the stands of their Colosseum-like ground, Stadio Filadelfia. The fans demanded passion and commitment befitting of their setting; the expectation was for the Torino players to fight for one another and for the pride of the shirt. If the Dutch model was, as Michels called it, an art, then Torino's approach was DIY. Michels, Cruyff and co planned their games in depth beforehand and decided the best way to approach each one. For Torino, it just happened. If an extra man was needed, he filled in dutifully. It was a mentality that was instilled in each of the players out of principle rather than plotting.

The fact that the Dutch were able to re-enact a style of play reminiscent of Torino's should not belittle the achievements of the Italians. Many of football's scholars believe that Torino provided the major building blocks for the creation of Total Football. In the wake of the Superga disaster Italian football needed a new style, as it now lacked the attacking control of Mazzola and his team-mates. The replacement was *Catenaccio*, literally translating as 'door-bolt'. It took the 'strength in numbers' approach of the great Torino side and moved it back, sitting deeper on the pitch, clogging the defence and stifling attacks. The style gave birth to a new position: the 'sweeper', who dropped into the space between the defence and the goalkeeper to, as the name suggests, sweep up any loose balls. It was a hugely frustrating system to play against and brought significant success to Italian

teams, none more so than Milan's Internazionale. The system did, however, require a spark of magic to ensure that games did not fizzle out into stolid, dour affairs. In the case of Internazionale, the man to provide this was none other than Valentino Mazzola's son Sandro, who played a similar role to the one his father had in *Il Grande Torino*. Mazzola and *Catenaccio* eventually led

Internazionale to the top of the European tree, culminating in a European Cup victory in 1964.

However, *Catenaccio* had an expiration date, as more attacking sides eventually worked out a way to penetrate the impenetrable. It came as no surprise that it was Rinus Michels' Ajax who managed to render the system obsolete once and for all. His side, featuring such talents as Johan Cruyff and Johan Neeskens (above), first defeated Inter Milan 2–0 in the 1972 European Cup final before routing fellow *Catenaccio* exponents AC Milan 6–0 in the second leg of the European Super Cup final the following year. It came as a bitter blow to the Italians, not only signalling the need for an overhaul but also giving a glimpse of just what Italian football could have become. Italy, a nation now synonymous with defensive football, could well have been a beacon of flair and overwhelming attacking dominance had Torino escaped the tragedy of 1949.

It is easy to dismiss claims that Torino were something special; so many great teams have come and gone, showing fleeting signs of excellence before dropping back to join the chasing pack. It was the timing of Torino's demise that made the events in the Superga hills even sadder from a footballing point of view. When Torino ruled the Italian game they had reached the peak. They could do no more than exact sustained and unerring domestic authority as they did between 1943 and 1949. They also won the Italian domestic cup, the Coppa Italia, in 1943 before it was suspended for fifteen years due to the destruction caused by the Second World War. Torino's supremacy was all the more concentrated as a result, since the league was the only trophy around. Had *Il Grande Torino* existed in a multi-competition era, their dominance could have been more widespread and the club's standing might well have survived the Superga tragedy.

Three years before the Coppa Italia returned to the Italian football calendar, a grander and more illustrious competition arrived. The European Cup was introduced into club football in 1955, giving the great and good of European club football a chance to go up against one another. For the first time, clubs were given a chance to compete against more than just their local rivals. However, it was initially less of a competition than a routine and inevitable crowning, as Spain's Real Madrid ran out victors in the first five seasons. Nobody could get close, and Real Madrid cemented the already firm foundation upon which they have built their near-unrivalled dynasty.

One team might just have been able to challenge the great Real Madrid sides. Of all the sides that might have stood a chance of toppling Madrid and breaking the still-unbeaten streak of five consecutive cups, Torino would have ranked among the strongest. This is not just baseless

Sandro Mazzola

speculation; Madrid themselves appreciated Torino as a noticeable absentee from the competition. And Madrid's talisman throughout the late 1950s and 60s, the Hungarian striker Ferenc Puskás, revered Valentino Mazzola long after his death. Madrid's tenure as European champions was ended in 1961 by Portuguese side Benfica, and they did not reach the final again until 1964. One team stood in their way: a Sandro Mazzola-led Internazionale. Inter ran out 3–1 winners, extending the barren spell for the Spanish giants. Far from bitter, Madrid accepted that they had been well beaten and Ferenc Puskás singled out one particular player for praise. With two goals to his name, Sandro Mazzola was approached by Puskás at the final whistle. 'I played against your father,' said Puskás. 'You did him proud and I want to give you my shirt.'

The Torino story is one of unfulfilled potential, though not for a lack of victories. The timing of their success and unfortunate demise was pivotal. Had they managed to avoid the Superga hillside that rainy day in 1949, Mazzola and his teammates would doubtlessly have gone on to become some of the best-known names in footballing history. They would most likely have taken home World Cup winner's medals and European Cups. As it is, the tale of Torino is one reserved for Italian fans to reminisce about, to recall the days when Stadio Filadelfia was a theatre for a footballing spectacle, rather than the run-down wasteland that it is today. Yet while Torino's great side never really received the global acclaim which they so truly deserved, their legacy was significant. Without their unrivalled team spirit and collaborative approach, the great sides that followed them would have lacked a vital inspiration. A decade of sublime supremacy in the Italian league bred a footballing philosophy that influenced the great Dutch sides of the 1970s, and in turn the great Barcelona sides ever since. The Torino approach continues to bear fruit, even if *Il Grande Torino* are not always credited.

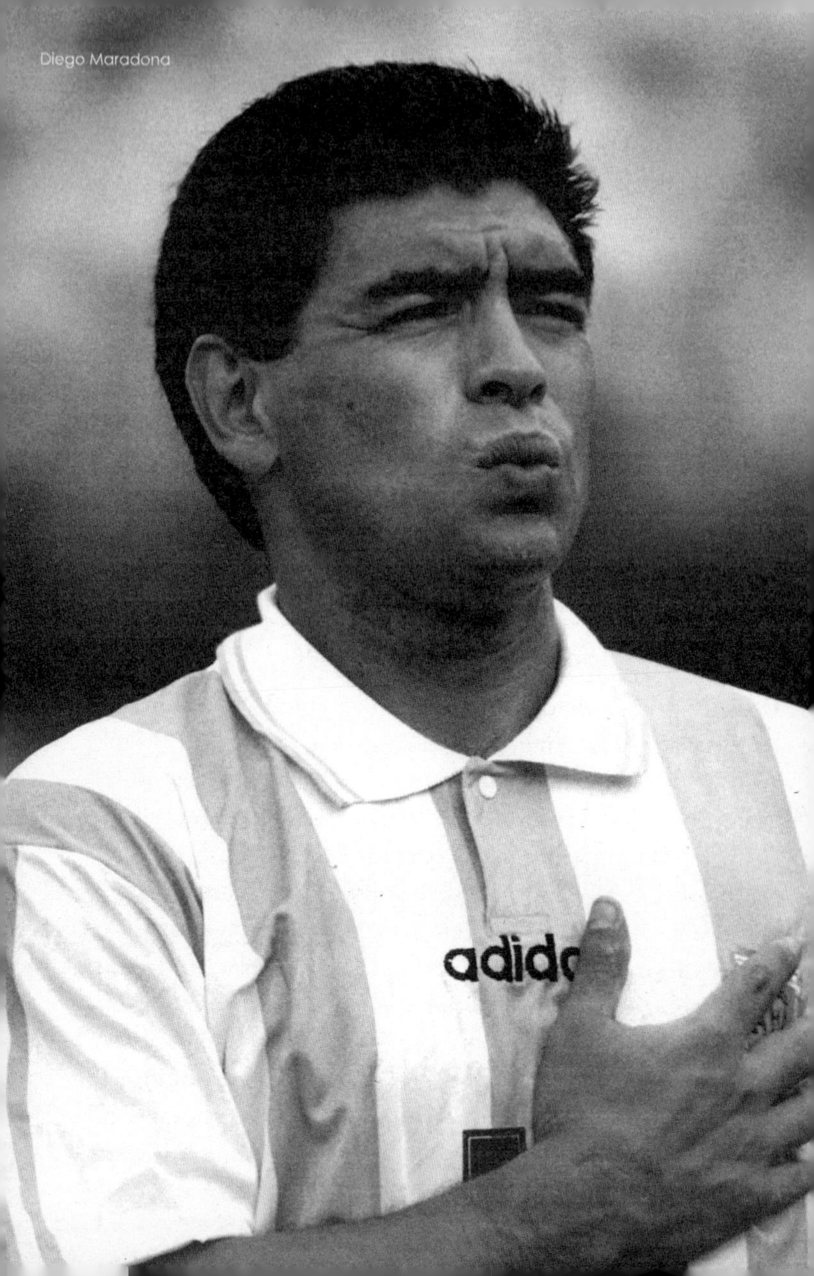

Diego Maradona

Chapter 7

Imagine that ...

An ephedrine-fuelled Maradona leads Argentina to glory in '94 ... and football's history books become worthless

USA 1994 was one of the most memorable World Cups in history. There are many reasons for this, but few of them are footballing ones. A tournament staged in stadia built with other sports in mind, it was always likely to feel slightly strange. The opening ceremony, for example, was one of the oddest exhibitions the sport had ever witnessed. As expected, the USA rolled out a number of high-profile celebrities to raise the curtain on the tournament. Oprah Winfrey played the role of host, but the appearance of Diana Ross has proven to be the enduring image. Dressed in red and white and flanked by dancers dressed in blue, she looked every inch the proud patriot as she energetically paraded around Soldier Field Stadium, Chicago. Midway through singing her hit single 'I'm Coming Out', Ross headed towards one end of the pitch. A ball was placed in front of her and she lined up a penalty kick. Showing the hallmarks of even the most accomplished spot-kick takers, she stuttered her run-up, trying to tempt the keeper into diving early. Her credentials were soon diminished, however, when she struck the ball wide of the goal as the special effects team triggered the goal frame to collapse. If this seemed bizarre, it was nothing compared to what followed over the next few weeks.

In the closing days of the tournament, the *Los Angeles Times* looked back on how the nation had staged the biggest show in football. The newspaper's assessment focused on the surrounding factors, exalting the Americanisms that had made the 1994 World Cup such a unique spectacle.

> They expected an athletic tournament. We staged a county fair, featuring nine exhibits stretched across 3,000 miles, with people and surroundings as varied as our twangs.

This was quite understandable and reflected the philosophy behind staging each World Cup in a different country, to expose and explore the ways in which different regions embrace the beautiful game. As far as attendance figures go, USA '94 is unrivalled. Even though the number of matches played in a typical tournament has increased from 52 in 1994 to 64 in recent years, no World Cup before or since has managed to top its total attendance of 3.59 million people. That is an average of just under 70,000 fans per match.

Soldier Field Stadium, Chicago

Stanford Stadium, California

As a result, the events of the month-long competition were magnified even more than one might expect a World Cup to be. Any high-profile controversies were bound to be scrutinised. Sadly there were two such controversies, darkening the legacy of what was otherwise a fondly remembered tournament. One came to its tragic conclusion outside the USA, a thousand or so miles south in Colombia. In a competitive if not formidable group that included hosts USA, Colombia struggled. They were eliminated following defeat by America, having played only two of their three group games. America took the lead when defender Andrés Escobar slid to cut out a cross and end an American attack, but inadvertently diverted the ball goalwards and beyond goalkeeper Oscar Cordoba. The game finished 2–1 but Escobar was blamed by many in Colombia for the defeat. After they had played their final game, beating Switzerland 2–0 in a dead rubber, they

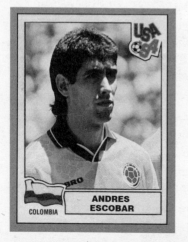

ANDRES
ESCOBAR

COLOMBIA

returned home. Less than a week later, Escobar was dead. In the early hours of 2 July he was approached by a group of men in the car park outside the El Indio bar in Medellín and shot repeatedly. Reports claimed that the gunmen had shouted '*Gol*' as they did so, leading many to the conclusion that the murder was carried out by a disgruntled betting syndicate.

The assassination of Andrés Escobar cast a brief shadow over the competition but, since the events had taken place outside the USA, and with so many people keen to make a success of the rest of the tournament, condolences were offered and the focus returned to the football. But another talking point proved more difficult to overlook. On the back of an anti-climactic second-place finish in 1990, Argentina returned to the world stage vying for glory. However, their presence at the tournament was by no means assured; they had undeniably been second-best in their qualifying group, finishing behind Escobar's Colombia and losing 5–0 to them in the process. As runner-up in the smaller of two South American qualifying groups, Argentina had to defeat Australia in a play-off match to seal their spot in USA '94. They made it, but only just, winning 2–1 on aggregate.

When the World Cup finally began, the majority of pundits rated Argentina's chances of triumphing as slim. Diego Maradona, Argentina's talisman in previous years, had fallen out of shape as a result of a turbulent personal life riddled with cocaine addiction and spiralling debts. He had won the Golden Ball award as player of the tournament when Argentina were victorious in 1986, and had received the bronze award in 1990. He had since left the highly competitive environs of Italy and the Napoli side in which he had prospered, returning to Argentina and relative international obscurity. So it came as a great surprise when, in the team's opening match of USA '94, Maradona seemed back to his best. Argentina were already two goals up in their opening game against Greece when a rapid short-passing move resulted in a thunderous shot from Maradona. It was as emphatic a strike as you could hope to see and Maradona, apparently full of adrenaline, ran towards a pitch-side cameraman in celebration. As he approached, a close-up of the goalscorer was relayed to millions across the globe. He roared into the camera, his mouth gaping and his eyes piercing.

Argentina went on to defeat Greece 4–0 and overcame Nigeria in their second game despite falling behind early on, but their tournament was about to be blown apart. After the Nigeria match Diego Maradona was approached by FIFA officials – more specifically, anti-doping officials. He tested positive for the performance-enhancing substance ephedrine. It was a devastating blow to Argentina's chances, but not an altogether unsuspected one. While Maradona's sparkling past made a simple return to form seem feasible, many onlookers had already grown suspicious of steroid abuse before FIFA acted. His celebration against Greece has long since been pointed to as an illustration of a chemically assisted player, so much so that the tale is often erroneously retold with Maradona being caught out after that particular game, instead of at the end of the following fixture. Nevertheless, the Argentine was sent packing and his teammates soon followed. They had already qualified for the knockout stages when their star departed, but defeat in the final group game

against Bulgaria was followed by a 3–2 loss to Romania in the last-sixteen round, and the void left by Maradona was clear for all to see.

The goal against Greece proved to be Maradona's last for Argentina, as the scandal of '94 brought down the curtain on an illustrious international career including 91 appearances, 34 goals and a World Cup winner's medal.

Maradona protested his innocence, claiming that it had been an honest mistake. He suggested that it had been the result of a mix-up over the differing contents of the Argentine and American versions of a sinus medicine for allergies. Yet in 2011, seventeen years on from his most shameful episode, he made allegations against Julio Grondona, the president of the Argentine Football Association. These claims suggested that the doping extended beyond the tournament in the USA, and with the knowledge of those in charge. Speaking to *The Football Show*, Maradona explained: 'What happened is that to play against Australia we were given a speedy coffee. They put something in the coffee and that's why we ran more.'

The implications of Maradona's claims were vast. On the most basic level, it suggested that Australia had been cheated out of a place in USA 1994. Although Argentina had little impact on the eventual outcome of the World Cup, as they did not face either finalist (Brazil or Italy), their absence would have shaken up the tournament considerably. The 24 nations that qualified for the competition's initial group stage were separated into four groups or 'pots'. With the rest of the pots dictated by geographical location, the most significant was Pot 1. This was made up of the five strongest nations and the hosts, in this case USA. The relative strength of the teams was measured by their FIFA world rankings, a points system based on their previous performances in qualifying and tournaments. As finalists in the two previous World Cups, this was the group Argentina was placed in. Australia, however, would not have made it into Pot 1. Had Argentina been removed from proceedings the shape of the World Cup would have altered dramatically as, in their absence, another nation of considerable strength would have stepped into their place and been afforded a better chance of success. The shake-up would have undoubtedly altered the fates of a number of nations, and possibly the identity of the eventual winners.

The significance of Maradona's doping stretches beyond the 1994 World Cup. As can be seen from his later allegations, his removal from the tournament was a case of damage limitation. In the end it was not FIFA that sent him on his way; instead Argentina dismissed him before FIFA had a chance to, hoping that their proactive stance would help them to avoid further punishments.

While Argentina's omission from the finals would have altered the competition, had they progressed further it might have changed the entire sport. In the aftermath of Maradona's failed drugs test, many people asked just how he had managed to participate in a second match at the tournament, considering his history of cocaine addiction, his striking performance and celebration in the opening game of the competition, and the resulting groundswell of speculation. The drugs tests were supposedly conducted on a random basis, so it was only by chance that Maradona's involvement ended when it did. In the group stages a certain amount of tinkering with the testing regime would have been possible, as FIFA president Sepp Blatter later explained. Two Argentines were tested for doping but only Maradona tested positive, but as Blatter suggested: 'If two players had been found guilty, FIFA probably would have changed the result.' Post-Maradona, the vanquished Greeks failed to win a single point in their group and Nigeria progressed ahead of Argentina, so Maradona's impact was ultimately superficial. However, if Maradona had led Argentina further into the tournament than he did, perhaps even to victory, then the ramifications would have been far greater.

Where doping has occurred in other sports, the same question is always raised – how do you rewrite the history books? In some sports, such as track athletics, it is relatively simple. Although the alarming performance may well have a psychological impact on the rest of the competitors, in running events the time of one sprinter is not logistically affected by their challengers. When Canadian 100m sprinter Ben Johnson was found guilty of doping at the Seoul Olympics in 1988, blaming the contents of a herbal drink in similar fashion to Maradona, he was stripped of a gold medal. Subsequently, the International Olympic Committee awarded gold to second-placed Carl Lewis, silver to third-placed Linford Christie and so on. However when it came out that cyclist Lance Armstrong had doped, the appropriate course of action was not so clear. Armstrong had dominated the sport's premier competition, the Tour de France, for almost a decade, triumphing repeatedly in the tactical endurance race. When news of his use of stimulants broke to the media in 2012 there were suggestions that it would spell the end of the sport in its high-profile and widely supported form. With its past built on what were essentially false results and achievements, it made the present seem meaningless and hollow. The same questions would have befallen the world of football had Maradona escaped detection in 1994.

It would be sensationalist to assert that football could be

brought down by a single drugs cheat; in fact, even widespread cheating would struggle to shatter the game. The World Cup, on the other hand, might not have coped quite so well. USA 1994 was the fifteenth-ever World Cup, and by this time it had long been established as the pinnacle of footballing competition. The form shown by Argentina with an ephedrine-fuelled Maradona at the helm was impressive. Aside from his goal in the opening game, he played a key role in the team's turnaround in the second fixture. This had also been his role in previous World Cups, orchestrating a strong but otherwise unremarkable side with admirable success. The team was built around him. Should he have managed to evade detection and continued to exert his influence upon the team, the integrity of the tournament would have been compromised. While in reality they exited to an unfancied Romanian side in the last sixteen, victory in that game would have pitted them against Sweden in the quarter-finals, one game shy of a match-up with tournament victors and bitter rivals Brazil.

There is of course no guarantee that Maradona would have been able to reverse the 3–2 defeat that Argentina suffered at the hands of Romania. Nor could one say with any certainty that they would have beaten Sweden in the following round. However, they would undoubtedly have been favourites with their inspirational forward in the side – especially with ephedrine running through his system. A semi-final against Brazil could have irreversibly changed the future of the World Cup. The previous year, Brazil and Argentina had gone head to head in the quarter-finals of

South America's primary international competition, the Copa América. The match finished 1–1 before Argentina prevailed 6–5 in a penalty shoot-out, en route to winning the tournament outright. A repeat of this outcome in the USA could have been a watershed moment in World Cup history. For Brazil to have been denied progression at the hands of a performance-enhanced Maradona would have made a mockery of the competition. Yet if Maradona's doping had been detected after such a fixture and Brazil reinstated at Argentina's expense, their eventual victory would have been tarred by a defeat, regardless of its unjust nature. The poisonous impact of Maradona's stimulants had the potential to render the whole tournament worthless, and with such a blot in the history books future World Cups would have taken place under its shadow.

Maradona has received a certain degree of leniency from the wider footballing community. The events of 1994 have been written off as unfortunate but ultimately inconsequential. Even his infamous handball goal against England in 1986, the 'Hand of God', which proved to be a deciding factor in Argentina's victorious World Cup campaign, was overlooked by many following the stunning solo effort he scored later in the same game. However, any further involvement in 1994 would probably have been a step too far even for his countless admirers, not just because of the harmful impact it would have had on one of sport's most beloved competitions but also because of the doubt it would have cast over his own career.

A knowing air is almost unavoidable when recounting

Maradona's involvement in '94. His poor form prior to the tournament, his previous cocaine convictions, the demonic celebration against Greece – all these elements make his doping seem obvious. Maradona's wildly unpredictable streak was used by many at the time to explain it away – a footballing genius turning on the style when it was least expected and most desired. If he had not been caught in 1994 he would probably not have been so open in 2011 about the qualifier against Australia. The revelations could have broken from elsewhere, and without the immediate isolation of the qualifying match and the two World Cup fixtures his entire career would have been cast under suspicion.

When news broke of Maradona's dismissal from USA 1994, Argentina was left in a state of disarray. Their hero had been caught cheating, their chances of success had evaporated and an illustrious international career had come to a shameful end. In his homeland, the sports editor at Argentine daily paper *Clarín*, Luis Vinker, said: 'People are in shock, they can't believe this has happened, but mostly they are sad.' There was little to be angry at, since they had witnessed the side without Maradona in their final two matches. His departure had not robbed them of anything; rather his presence early on had provided them with something that was not legitimately theirs in the first place. Perhaps the sadness would have turned to anger if they had faced retrospective elimination against Brazil, but the comparatively low-key nature of the consequences meant that the nation was simply reminded of the star they had lost.

The whole sorry episode had the potential to sully the good name of football and the FIFA World Cup for years to come, but ultimately came to be seen as evidence that cheats never prosper. This philosophy is of course verging on naïve and, as can be seen by the destructive wake left by drug cheats in other sports, football got away extremely lightly.

Chapter 8

Imagine that ...

Honduras rout El Salvador in 1970 World Cup qualifiers ... and a brutal conflict is avoided

> Football has nothing to do with fair play. It is bound up
> with hatred, jealousy, boastfulness, disregard of all rules
> and sadistic pleasure in witnessing violence: in other
> words it is war minus the shooting.

These are the words of George Orwell, a poetic if rather
negative assessment of the game of football. It is an excerpt
from his 1945 essay 'The Sporting Spirit', but could just
as easily have come from the pages of *Nineteen Eighty-four*,
so oppressive and dystopian is the tone. Nonetheless it
stands as a highly provocative argument. While thousands
would agree wholeheartedly with Orwell's view, thousands
more would argue that fair play and the spirit of war are
not mutually exclusive. If two teams sign up to battle on

the pitch, are the realms of fair play not dictated by their willingness to compete? Orwell's fellow wordsmith and one-time professional goalkeeper Albert Camus valued football somewhat more highly, stating: 'All I know most surely about morality and obligations, I owe to football.' Yet even the most fervent advocate of the merits of the game cannot deny that there are times when the sport crosses the line between moral validity and barbarity. In 1969 this line was crossed in the most dramatic of fashions.

At the time a great deal of tension existed between the neighbouring Central American nations of Honduras and El Salvador. In terms of population El Salvador was by far the larger, with over 3 million recognised nationals compared to Honduras's 2.3 million. However, while El Salvador's population was compacted into a nation of only 8,000 square miles, the people of Honduras were spread across a country more than five times the size. The overcrowding of El Salvador led thousands to cross the border in search of a greater quality of life, much to the anger of the Hondurans. It was estimated that at the peak of the migration around 300,000 Salvadorans inhabited the land of their neighbours. Bitter arguments ensued, with El Salvador pleading for the borders to be altered to grant them more land. Border disputes rarely conclude amicably and this one was no different. As El Salvador continued to argue its case, Honduras predictably set about controlling the influx of Salvadorans through eviction, an act which only served to aggravate matters.

This is where football comes in. With relations between the two nations at an all-time low and the 1970 World Cup

looming, qualification had reached the final stages. Both El Salvador and Honduras had managed to emerge from their preliminary groups, only to be paired together in a two-game semi-final. Unusually, this was structured in such a way that only the overall outcomes – wins, draws and losses – would determine who progressed; the aggregate scoreline was not significant. The first match was to be played in Honduras with the return fixture scheduled a week later in El Salvador. Not only did this present the potential for on-pitch fallings-out, it also gave cause for thousands of supporters to cross the border, placing further stress on the relationship.

The first match appeared to be drawing towards a stalemate, perhaps the most desirable outcome for the sake of peace. However, as the game strayed into injury time, the home side found a late winner – Honduras 1–0 El Salvador. Riots erupted as the Salvadorans protested the outcome, claiming the match should have already ended; the referee's interpretation of injury time differed to that of the travelling fans. But all was not lost. If El Salvador could win their home tie, they would avoid exit. When Honduras crossed the border for the second match the rioting began downtown long before the match, with three Salvadoran fatalities. After two people had been killed outside their hotel, the Honduras team was relocated to an undisclosed location for their own safety, later revealed to be the Honduran embassy.

Inside the ground things were comparatively peaceful. Stringent policing measures ensured that both sets of fans were well marshalled throughout. The effects of the disruptions the previous night were clear for all to see as a weary Honduras succumbed to a resounding 3–0 Salvadoran victory. There was to be no repeat of the dramatic controversy that had sparked unrest at the end of the previous match. Rather than bemoan the defeat, Honduras' coach spoke of his relief shortly after the match: 'We're awfully lucky that we lost, otherwise we wouldn't be alive today.' The disquiet outside was immediately reignited post-match, however, with Honduran fans pelted with missiles as they filtered back to their homeland. A conclusion had not been reached, either on or off the pitch. With their ire increased by the post-match attacks, the Hondurans increased pressure on the Salvadorans to exit their country. Meanwhile, the football would enter into a third and final match, a decider to be played in Mexico City. Despite removing the need for either set of fans to set foot on the land of their opponent, it still provided an unwanted focal point and a chance for further dispute. The rest of Central and South America looked on as the two nations battled it out.

The deciding match was a characteristically unpredictable affair. With El Salvador leading for most of the match, Honduras forced extra time with an 89th-minute equaliser. They then proceeded to take the lead before El Salvador exacted their revenge, scoring twice in injury time to claim victory and advance to the final qualifying stage. It was the most inflammatory outcome imaginable. After three gruelling battles and a whole host of dramatic late twists, Honduras were humiliated. They had been dealt the most crushing

blow by their bitterest foes; the very men they felt were forcing them out of work and invading their homeland.

Within hours of the final whistle came the inevitable
fall-out. El Salvador and Honduras severed diplomatic ties,
beginning a rapid descent into chaos as border skirmishes
erupted. Within three weeks the two nations were at war.
On 14 July 1969, the Salvadoran Air Force took to the skies
with Honduras locked firmly in their sights. A hundred
hours of bloody and costly conflict followed and the death
toll soon reached the thousands, mainly Honduran civil-
ians. Finally, after four days, pressure from the Honduran
authorities and the surrounding nations led to a cease-
fire, but it would be decades before the two nations truly
resolved their differences.

The situation in El Salvador and Honduras in 1969 was
obviously a complex and fragile one. When the two nations
were drawn together in World Cup qualification it was
tantamount to dousing an already overstocked tinderbox
in petrol. It would only require the smallest spark or injury-
time controversy to send it up in flames.

With so much ill feeling between the two nations it would
be easy to assume that conflict was unavoidable, and the
football incidental. Yet over those three weeks the ongoing
conflicts were concentrated in a volatile environment that
only football could provide: heated, immediate, tribal. Not

just competition but knockout competition. The nature of the matchup dictated that one side would be lauded as victors, the other branded losers. In the long run there could be no draw, no amicable resolution. The prize of victory would be strung out over the course of a number of months should the victor overcome the last obstacle, in the form of Haiti, and reach the finals in Mexico – as El Salvador did. One clear question arises from the conflict, an anomaly that seems counterintuitive. If El Salvador won, why did *they* begin the conflict?

One might have expected the fallen Hondurans to mete out their swift retaliation as El Salvador began their celebrations but, as we now know, the opposite occurred. Riding the momentum of their sporting victory, El Salvador saw a chance to capitalise on their temporary and unprecedented dominance in the region. Their victory march stretched all the way from Mexico City to the heart of Honduras. It was evident from looking at their aircraft that their strike was impulsive. It had been no secret that El Salvador lacked military might and that the Hondurans possessed far superior means. This was very much a function of El Salvador's overcrowding, since the nation's financial resources were distributed among an unmanageable population. However, when disharmony between the neighbouring nations escalated during the World Cup qualifiers, the US imposed an arms embargo upon both countries. This was a great leveller, forcing both sides to source their weaponry more creatively. The result was the recycling of archaic Second World War piston-engine aircraft and rudimentary artillery attachments. With Honduras hampered by the same restrictions, El Salvador realised that they would have no better chance in conflict

than at that moment, so they flew their cobbled-together air force deep into Honduras before beginning the real assault on foot, storming the borders. Football hadn't just riled the two nations, it had created a military situation that passively encouraged El Salvador to attack – a 'now or never' situation if ever there was one.

The conflict might well have been postponed, if not avoided, had the result of the World Cup qualifier been different. Relations between any two sets of fans would have been tested by the topsy-turvy nature of the three-legged semi-final, especially with the late drama heaped on. With two nations already on the brink of conflict, and two sets of fans so determined to secure bragging rights and a spot in the World Cup finals, premature celebrations and dented pride provided a catalyst for war. Although any remotely inflammatory incident at any stage could have sparked the ensuing riots, if the first of the three matches had been a more one-sided then the war might not have followed with such crushing inevitability. Amid the unrest that followed Honduras' late winner, it would be eighteen days until any further controversy would be played out. The return leg was rendered a procession in predictability, with the Hondurans too tired from their night in the embassy, and too scared to upset the baying crowds.

Of course a Honduras defeat would have left the El Salvadorans far happier, but their later attack proved that a happy El Salvador was not necessarily a peaceful one. More intriguing is what might have happened had Honduras won the first leg more convincingly. In footballing terms the 1–0 lead they took from the first leg should have secured them a vital advantage, but the riots turned it into a burden. If Honduras had managed to pierce the Salvadoran defence earlier in their home tie, then the outrage of their defeated opponents would have been replaced by disheartenment and disappointment. The Salvadorans would have had no grounds on which to consider the goal illegitimate and as a result their collective anger would have been sapped, most likely sparing the ensuing riots. The fact that the two games were not decided by an aggregate scoreline, but rather an unusual two-team league system, meant that the second game was always going to hold meaning, regardless of what had happened in the first. Without the first-leg controversy, when Honduras crossed the border seven days later they would not have been greeted with quite the same vitriol, allowing them to avoid relocation to their embassy.

On the pitch, it is difficult to gauge which team was the stronger. Honduras may have lost overall, but openly declared fears for their safety after the second and third fixtures. In the one match that was contested under relatively even conditions they were late winners. Of course there is no guarantee that they would have replicated the victory in front of a partisan El Salvador crowd, even after a good night's sleep and minus the precedent for rioting. Home advantage so often tells in football and Honduras may well still have succumbed to their hosts. But this was not just another game. Form and expectations were secondary to national momentum. Such was the inseparabil-

ity of football and national pride at the time that a more routine opening victory for Honduras could have led to despondency in the Salvadoran camp. As it happened, the perceived injustice of the first leg made victory all the more vital to them in the return fixture. Without this burning sense of unfairness, El Salvador might not have created such a formidable environment for the fixture, both inside and outside the ground.

The collective calming of tempers would only have benefited Honduras. In retrospect, if El Salvador had to lose the first leg, they could not have lost in a more productive way. Their fury powered them to victory and a debut appearance in a World Cup. Without this propulsion they would have been a far less daunting opposition and Honduras would have been in a stronger position to capitalise on their positive start to the tie. Honduras did not require a second victory to progress – a draw would have sufficed due to the points system. The effect of this would have been colossal. The missiles which rained down upon Honduran fans following their 3–0 defeat are unlikely to have been thrown had they won both legs comfortably. It was a backlash born of the frustration of the first leg, a bitter taunt from the Salvadorans who would otherwise have been left ruing a comprehensive defeat.

Above all, the bitter sporting battle would not have entered into a third match, a third country and a fourth week. The two nations would have been able to return their focus to the complex political matters that divided them, rather than have their minds clouded by the irrational immediacy of football. The short-lived war was so brief because it was not part of any long-term strategy. It was reactive and avoidable. Without the footballing backdrop conflict might well still have occurred, but it would undoubtedly have been more measured, necessary and most likely far less costly in terms of Honduran civilian casualties. It was a hugely regrettable 100-hour period in the history of Honduras and El Salvador, but with a slightly different outcome on the pitch George Orwell's belief that football is 'war minus the shooting' need never have been proved wrong.

Chapter 9

Imagine that ...

Messi is unable to afford growth hormone treatment ... and Spanish football loses its charitable nature

As the Argentine prodigy Lionel Messi (pictured left) rapidly rose through Barcelona's youth ranks at the start of the 21st century, few failed to be seduced by his talents. With sublime close control, an unfeasibly low centre of gravity and immaculate finishing, those fortunate enough to have witnessed his beginnings claim that it was clear even then that Messi was special. However, some were not convinced, including one Frank de Boer. Having spent two successful seasons at Barcelona, de Boer has a better understanding than most of the qualities required to be a success at the club. In 2010, after the Argentine had collected his second Ballon d'Or award as Europe's best performer over the course of the previous year, de Boer admitted that he had previously doubted Messi's potential to scale such heights.

His concerns, he explained, had emerged at a youth tournament five years earlier to which he had accompanied Barcelona's manager at the time, Frank Rijkaard:

> Frank kept raving about him because he was already at Barcelona but I didn't think he played a great tournament. I told Frank that he was trying to do too much and wasn't focused enough. I said he needed to play more as a team player.

In the years since, Messi has created a role that is all his own, managing to do what de Boer considered to be 'too much' with alarming success.

De Boer's concerns were understandable; few players manage to cope with the burden of duties under which Messi thrives. His success was far from a sure thing, but the battle he faced was against very different limitations to those de Boer had in mind. By the age of eleven Messi was standing out among his teammates at his club in Argentina, Newell's Old Boys, but was also diagnosed with a career-threatening condition – growth hormone deficiency (GHD). At eleven years of age he could cope due to the still-diminutive build of his opponents, but that would change in time. Without growth hormone treatment he stood no chance of ever being able to compete at the highest level. Doctors priced up a course of treatment at nearly $1,000 a month, a sum which was quite simply unaffordable for Messi's parents, who had three other children to provide for. The only hope was to find a club willing to foot the bill for him.

Messi's reputation was already well established nationally and scouts were a familiar sight at Newell's youth fixtures, so there was no shortage of interested parties. Among the sides contemplating Messi was River Plate, Argentina's most successful club. It would have represented a significant step up for Messi but the club concluded that the outlay on medical bills was too big a risk to take on a boy who was not even fourteen at the time. There was always a chance that, even if the treatment did allow Messi to develop sufficiently, injury or a loss of form could prevent them from ever seeing a return on such a large investment. As River Plate's hesitancy revealed, even the top sides in Argentina could not afford to take the gamble.

It came as a huge relief when global heavyweights Barcelona invited the frustrated youngster for a trial. He travelled with his family to deepest Catalunya and set about winning himself a future in the game. The coaches watched in awe as Messi weaved his way through the tightly knit defences of their youth teams, consisting of some of the most promising prospects in football. The decision was unanimous and Messi was offered a contract which he gladly signed. In later years he would speak of the simplicity of the decision he had faced:

> It wasn't difficult for me to move to Barcelona because I knew I had to. I needed money for my medicine to help me grow and Barcelona were the only club that offered. So as soon as they did, I knew I had to go.

Considering that Messi is now considered to be one of the greatest players ever to play the game, the suggestion that his career could have fizzled out in his teenage years seems almost absurd. At age thirteen, Messi had been ineligible to sign a professional contract at Newell's Old Boys, therefore Barcelona were not required to pay a single peseta in transfer fees to acquire him. As bargains go, there are few better.

His development at Barcelona was meteoric. Already equipped with impeccable attacking skills, the course of treatment meant that he soon had a body capable of using these assets. The only worrying side effect was that the rapid growth spurt outpaced his stamina and so he suffered from fatigue, but endurance training enabled him to overcome this. The reduced capacity for running did little to hide his talents, as the stars of Barcelona's first team quickly noticed their soon-to-be teammate. Ronaldinho (below), the club's leading performer at the time, expressed an early admi-

ration for Messi's talents: 'When he came to train with the first team when he was still very young I already noticed that he was different and that with time he would become a big star.' Unbeknown to Ronaldinho, the youngster would eventually usurp him as Barcelona's main man, taking his coveted number 10 shirt in the

process, although the two maintained a strong friendship. Messi had a lot to thank Ronaldinho for, not least his first goal, coming in the Camp Nou in May 2005. With Barcelona already a goal up against Albacete and with 87 minutes on the clock, the game appeared to be all but over when Messi made his way on to the pitch. But he had other ideas. Winning the ball with his back to goal, Messi laid it off to Ronaldinho before spinning and running into the box. The two players linking up in a manner reminiscent of time-worn partnership, Ronaldinho proceeded to loft the ball over the defence before Messi confidently lobbed the goalkeeper. It was exactly the type of cool finish that the Barcelona fans would witness hundreds of times over the following seasons.

The career of Lionel Messi has been one of the most phenomenal and record-breaking in the history of football. The
fatigue that nagged throughout his early days at Barcelona
faded, as did the injuries that stalled his breakthrough. In
the space of a decade, Messi has transitioned from a feeble,
underdeveloped boy into a true athlete. In the 2011/12
season he managed to play in 60 games across six separate
tournaments at both club and international level, scoring
a staggering 72 goals. It was more than any individual has
ever scored in a single season, beating a pre-war record of 70
set in America. He shows no signs of slowing down either, as
in 2012 he broke German striker Gerd Müller's long-standing record for the most goals in a calendar year, scoring 91
times – six more than Müller's 1972 total of 85. Yet for all
of this he could have just as easily found himself plying his
trade as a skilful but stoppable showman in South America,
an admirable but insignificant existence compared to the
one he boasts today.

10

It is often said of individuals that they were born in the
wrong era and that their talents would have been better
appreciated in a different period. This is not an assertion
often made of Lionel Messi. When Messi arrived in Barcelona the stage was set for a big and sustained entrance to the
game. What is more, Messi found himself in the one country
that was the most conducive to his style of play, completely

by chance. It was only as a result of his desperate need to fund his growth hormone treatment that Messi left his native Argentina at such a young age, a move he probably would not have made had it not been essential for his career.

In the early days at Barcelona he suffered badly from homesickness. When the chance to relocate to Spain had arisen the Messis had jumped at the chance, realising just how vital it could prove in Lionel's development. However, they arrived with no knowledge of the city and were even surprised to learn that it was on the coast. His mother and siblings were unable to settle in their new surroundings and soon returned to their home in Rosario, Argentina; Lionel stayed on in Barcelona, accompanied by his father, Jorge. This turbulent time could so easily have seen Messi give up and return to his homeland but instead he persevered, living only for football as he rose through the ranks at the club's *La Masia* academy. He was following in the footsteps of some of the club's greatest talents, namely the likes of Xavi Hernández and Andres Iniesta; players who, like the academy's new recruits, now look up to Messi themselves. Few clubs in world football have such an organic ethos, opting to produce their own talents instead of buying in established stars from their rivals. This trend has become even more deliberate since Messi emerged. Of course, the Argentine was not technically a home-grown player, but with the bulk of his footballing education coming from Barcelona he seems like one. He has become the exemplary product of an already esteemed production line, and without him Barcelona's home-grown approach might have faltered.

With Messi leading the way, Barcelona have transformed from one of the best teams on earth to arguably the greatest team in history. As is often the case when a side surpasses their rivals in such imperious fashion, Barcelona took a different approach to other clubs on the pitch as well as off it. While all their rivals were building teams full of tall, muscled athletes, the Spaniards opted for a more technical approach. Even after hormone treatment Messi only stands at five feet seven inches; but he does not look out of place among his teammates. Xavi is the same height, so too Iniesta. Most of their players are less than six feet tall. They have adapted their style of play to suit their diminutive stature, in the process perfecting *tiki-taka*, the Spanish passing game that has taken the world by storm. Consisting of relentless short floor-bound passes, *tiki-taka* is aesthetically pleasing and aims to exhaust the opposition by dominating possession with quick, accurate exchanges. It was first introduced to the academy by Dutch footballing legend Johan Cruyff in the late 1980s, but the club could not completely rely on it until Messi came along; now other

clubs seek to emulate it. As a result, academies across the globe have changed their focus from physicality to technical coaching, altering the whole sport. Young players who would once have been turned away for being too slight are now much coveted, whereas the attributes of stronger, taller players are less appreciated.

Messi's impact upon Barcelona has also been felt off the pitch. Football is increasingly powered by money and sponsorship deals. In addition to his footballing excellence, Messi enjoys a lifestyle that is quiet and uncontroversial compared to that of most footballers. A clean-living individual at the peak of his profession, any brand would love to be associated with him. And he has reaped the rewards. In June 2012, business magazine *Forbes* revealed Messi's

earnings over the previous twelve months, both from club salary and individual sponsorship deals. The details were startling. With almost a 50:50 split between the two income sources, at the tender age of 25 he was making just under £25 million a year. Sponsorship money came from companies such as Adidas, PepsiCo, Herbalife and Dolce & Gabanna, among others.

Although these deals are impressive measures of his financial value, it was a Messi-driven club sponsorship deal that made clear his unrivalled worth.

Barcelona's club motto is *Més que un club*: 'More than a club'. It is a reference to its proud Catalan roots, exemplified by their desire to nurture home-grown stars – players who understand the culture of Barcelona. There is no more iconic symbol of the club's heritage than the famous blue and burgundy kit, known locally as the *blaugrana*. In an attempt to preserve their unique traditions, the club refused to sell sponsorship space on their shirts when this became common in the late 1970s, and, unusually, maintained the ban well into the 21st century. Further to this, when they finally did free up space on their shirts for advertising, it was not to secure multi-million-euro sponsorship for the club. Instead, in September 2006, Barcelona pledged to donate an annual sum to international children's charity UNICEF and in turn display its logo on their shirts. It was an admirable and widely praised move from the club, providing great publicity for both the club and the charity.

However, by 2011 Barcelona's financial situation had weakened considerably. A culture of financial misman-

agement blighted the club and the wage bill had become unmanageable. The club had two options: sell players or sell shirt space. The sale of one player in particular could have helped the club to finance the rest of its stars for a number of seasons; but naturally the club was not prepared to sell Messi, the best player of a generation, at any price. As a result, having taken out a loan of £120 million the year before to stave off the inevitable, in December 2010 the club agreed a sponsorship deal with non-profit organisation the Qatar Foundation, whose logo moved that of UNICEF to the back of the shirt. Netting the club £148 million over the next five years, it was the largest ever deal of its type in football and was made both possible and necessary by Lionel Messi's presence at the club. It was a deal that angered many of the club's supporters, not least Johan Cruyff, the man who had arguably laid the foundations for Messi's progress. 'By selling the shirt it shows me that we are not being creative, and that we have become vulgar,' said Cruyff. 'If things are so bad, then we should cut out the deal we have with UNICEF, and all the values it represents, because we pay them to carry the logo on our shirts.' Many agreed with him.

Although Cruyff's suggestion of calling time on the UNICEF deal highlighted the strength of feeling about the sponsorship deal, in reality it would not have helped. The club paid roughly £1.6 million a year to the charity, a drop in the ocean compared to the rest of their debts and the resulting Qatar Foundation deal. Had the club sold Messi, they would have been considerably weaker on the

pitch and so missed out on vital prize money from competitions, along with the unmatched demand for shirt sales with 'Messi 10' printed on the back. In reality even if the club had sold its most valuable asset, it would merely have staved off the need for sponsorship for a few more years; and without Messi at the club, sponsorship would have been worth far less. The salaries that got Barcelona into financial difficulties, not least that of Lionel Messi, were a product of the wider market and as their rivals funded wage bills with sponsorship, Cruyff's idealistic approach would always have been unsustainable.

In the end, Messi's presence at the world's biggest club enabled payments to UNICEF to continue. It also kept him in the spotlight, making the Leo Messi Foundation possible. The foundation reflects the difficult beginning of Messi's journey to superstardom, funding medical centres for children with conditions including but not limited to growth hormone deficiency and assisting with the additional costs that can otherwise make treatment unaffordable, such as travel and accommodation for the families of sick children. He has also personally footed the medical bill for a Moroccan youngster, Waleed Kashash, who requires a similar course of treatment to the one Barcelona paid for Messi to undergo as a child. Lasting six years, the treatment costs are expected to exceed £30,000 by the end of the course. It may be a small sum when compared to Messi's earnings, but it would otherwise be unaffordable for Kashash's family, as would it have been for Messi if not for Barcelona's investment.

Lionel Messi continues to forge a quite remarkable career on the pitch, and will probably be regarded by most as the world's greatest ever player when he eventually retires. But his work off the pitch has been even more impressive. Barcelona's charitable legacy would have suffered had they decided not to take a chance on the small boy from Rosario. They would most likely have sold their stars to stave off the threat of shirt sponsorship for another year or two, and the UNICEF partnership may well have fallen foul of the fans' outrage. But with Messi in the team, they have a player worth selling shirt space for. It is much better to sell shirt space than Messi, as UNICEF, the Qatar Foundation and children everywhere like Waleed Kashash will attest.

Chapter 10

Imagine that ...

Robben Island remains a
football-free zone ... and the
leaders of the anti-apartheid
movement remain immobilised

When the World Cup came to South Africa in the summer
of 2010, it was inevitable that the nation's chequered past
would be revisited. The national team, affectionately known
as *Bafana Bafana* (Zulu for 'the boys'), had been banned
from the competition between 1958 and 1992 due to FIFA's
opposition to the apartheid regime. However, despite South
Africa being shunned by the international community,
football remained a vital part of life there, not least for the
prisoners of Robben Island.

Situated five and a half miles off the shore of Cape Town,
Robben Island is now a World Heritage Site and one of
South Africa's most-visited tourist attractions. Over 1,000
people a day visit the island by ferry. The tourists do not
come for the views, although on a clear day these can be

quite spectacular. They come to hear the stories of the prisoners who were held there – the anti-apartheid activists – and of the leper colony before it. Once part of the mainland, erosion has since cut the island adrift and it now stands alone, the perfect reminder of the colossal struggles of Nelson Mandela and his peers.

The apartheid regime, a system of racial segregation, was in place from 1948 until 1994. To suppress any backlash, the government imprisoned the leaders of their political opposition on Robben Island, and the pre-existing contingent of non-political prisoners soon came to be vastly outnumbered. Here they endured a gruelling regime of physically demanding work, an oppressive schedule designed to sap any energy for revolt. Food was scarce and prisoners were subjected to intrusive and humiliating searches on a daily basis. In some cases cells accommodated three times the recommended number of inmates. Prisoners longed for anything that would allow them even the briefest escape from their reality. In an attempt to satisfy this desire, in 1964 the inmates launched a widespread and long-running campaign. Every week a different prisoner would approach the warders with a simple request – bring football to Robben Island. The decision to share the duty was not cowardly, nor was it a display of unity, but was rather a defence mechanism. Asking had consequences and prisoners were routinely punished for their audacity. Had the burden of the campaign fallen upon one individual's shoulders, it would not have lasted long.

Much to everyone's surprise, after three years of rebuffals, in 1967 the warders relented. One of the rights afforded to prisoners was contact with the Red Cross; they could make requests and raise concerns, and the organisation would attempt to address them on the inmates' behalf. So, with the help of the Red Cross, the Makana Football Association was founded. It was named by prisoners after a warrior prophet who himself had been imprisoned on the island in the 1800s, and who sadly drowned trying to escape. Football, or *diski* as it is known in the townships, was coming to Robben Island and the prisoners readied themselves for its arrival. The first task was to set up teams. It emerged that the jailers had only given in to the inmates' petitioning because they saw the opportunity to nurture rivalries among prisoners. The inaugural Makana football league was contested by seven sides consisting solely of prisoners –

the warders wanted nothing to do with it. In keeping with the authorities' 'divide and rule' agenda, the teams were not simply clusters of unaffiliated men but groups based on political beliefs. All except for one. The Manong team was a free house, open to any player who could not relate to any of the other six, an eclectic approach at odds with the apartheid regime.

As expected, the league was very well received, attracting many players and fans. Before long the seven teams essentially became clubs, complete with reserve teams, and in time further leagues were required to satisfy the increased number of willing participants and differing standards. Suddenly the prisoners had something meaningful to think about. There was a focal point to life on the island, something more fulfilling than just splitting rocks mindlessly day after day. In time the pre-existing divisions on the island, rather than being exacerbated, became muted. The split between advocates of the Pan Africanist Congress (PAC) and the African National Congress (ANC) weakened as the opposing parties were able to resolve at least some of their differences on the field of play. Such was the overwhelming power of football on Robben Island that the prison authorities began to fight against it. They would announce, without reason or notice, that there would be no football that week. Sporadic, unpredictable and crushing blows were dealt to prisoners until all they could do was revolt. They wanted to play football but only on their terms; it was a matter of principle that they were not prepared to see compromised. After much discussion, the prisoners decided that they

would boycott the league. On a week when the guards decided to allow football, the prisoners simply refused to play, responding with the same words that were used to deprive them: 'No football today'. The football may have gone, but inmates were united like never before. The stand-off lasted for an entire year, ending only when the guards on the island were replaced. In 1968 the league returned, stronger than ever.

The Makana Football Association was far from the ramshackle set-up one might expect to exist under such circumstances. The equipment was primitive but painstakingly prepared, with boots fashioned out of women's shoes with the heels removed and old tyres used as a hardwearing sole. The kits were in vibrant colours, as is the tradition in African football, with the complex and much-loved team badges drawn on each individual shirt. The league was well-organised, holding monthly meetings complete with

minute-taking. There is a display dedicated to these details at the port where visitors board ferries to Robben Island. The port itself is named after one of the island's most famous residents: the Nelson Mandela Gateway.

Mandela, however, was unable to participate in the Makana football leagues. Incarcerated in an isolation wing, his only experience of football on Robben Island was the glimpses of games he saw through the bars of his cell window. Nevertheless, he had been active in the initial campaign, selflessly contributing to a cause he was never likely to benefit from. That said, every prisoner did benefit; so did South Africa as a whole. In an environment devoid of morality and justice, the prisoners of Robben Island were able to wrestle back some semblance of a human right, sending a powerful message to the rest of the nation.

When considering the brutal hardship of life on Robben Island, it is easy to jump to the conclusion that football was replaceable. Any light-hearted release in such surroundings would surely have been appreciated by prisoners. However, it was essential that the recreational focus was a sporting one; nothing else would have provided an outlet for the physical strength the prisoners had gained from their gruelling manual labour. As the nation's most popular sport, football united the prisoners, even those like Mandela who were barred from participating.

The only 'crime' most of the prisoners had committed was to oppose the apartheid regime. These weren't untrustworthy individuals, nor were they feckless or outcasts. Back home they had been community leaders, fighting bitterly against oppression. The apartheid government were certainly right to think that removing these individuals from South African society would lessen the threat they posed to the regime, but they did not realise that storing all such individuals together on one island would lead to their own eventual downfall. Tony Suze, a youth member of the Pan Africanist Congress and a one-time Robben Island inmate, later told of the mobilising power of football at the prison: 'As long as it had to do with football, we were able to tell the authorities how we wanted it, why we wanted it and so on and they would listen. That was an expression of some kind of freedom for us.' Although football mattered a great deal to the prisoners – indeed some results were so hotly disputed that they risked causing acrimony – it was the accompanying discourse that made it the springboard for revolution.

With football alive on the island, requests for additional sports were consequently made, considered and in many cases accepted. Special allowances were granted so that football schedules would not be disrupted. The Makana Football Association was nothing to do with the prison warders; it was the brainchild of the politically minded prisoners. Once they had been granted their wish, they knew that forming a governing body would make it easier for them to discuss other issues with their jailors. It satisfied the needs of the authorities and empowered inmates all at the same time, something that could not be achieved in any other aspect of prison life. Without it, the present political landscape of South Africa would be vastly different.

The higher echelons of South African politics have been filled with ex-Robben Islanders since 1990. They have not all followed the same political path, being divided primarily by the split between the African National Congress (ANC) and Pan Africanist Congress (PAC) parties. Nelson Mandela's legacy is obvious. Less well known is the fact that Jacob Zuma, the nation's president from 2009, also resided on the island, along with former defence minister Terror Lekota and the charismatic business leader and host of South Africa's 2005 version of *The Apprentice*, Tokyo Sexwale.

Except for Mandela, they were all keen participants in the Makana football league. These are just a famous handful of the league's successful political exports; many lesser-known members have played a hugely influential role in South Africa's post-apartheid resurgence. Robben Island, once a prison for the country's most powerful activists, has since been the uniting experience of the ANC and PAC parties' leaders. The result of this shared hardship has been a far more harmonious relationship between the two, something that simply would not have been possible without football. Arguments that threatened to spill over in the cells and quarries were instead settled on the field.

Sport's influence on the South African government did not end with the Makana league. Many of the proudest moments of South Africa's post-apartheid history have been sporting ones. In 1995, a pivotal time for the nation, South Africa hosted the Rugby World Cup. Although apartheid regulations and segregation had been abolished five years earlier, the government of F.W. de Klerk did not leave office until 1994 when it was replaced by Nelson Mandela and the ANC. As president during the Rugby World Cup, Mandela exerted a powerful influence upon the country's approach to the tournament. The national rugby team, known as the Springboks, had long been a whites-only setup and the focus of much ire from black South Africans. However, rather than shun the team as an icon of apartheid values, Mandela saw an opportunity to reconcile. He arranged to meet the Springboks' team captain Francois Pienaar and set about rehabilitating the national team in the whole nation's eyes.

The public obeyed Mandela's call and provided the over-whelming home support that powered the Springboks to victory. The competition was heralded as the birth of the Rainbow Nation, black and white South Africans united in the most unlikely of contexts. It was a feat that reverberated around the world. Since the transition out of apartheid had been gradual and blurred, the World Cup introduced the new South Africa to the watching world. A government that had been mobilised by sport reaped its benefits once more. The values of sport and its power to unite have dominated South Africa's post-apartheid mentality. The 1995 Rugby World Cup was just one example of sport being used to

improve South Africa's image in the eyes of the world. This was particularly necessary because of the depths to which it had sunk. In the late 1950s, football in South Africa had been consigned to the doldrums. After it emerged that the nation's law would prevent it from selecting a mixed-race team to take part in international competitions, FIFA banned them until the law was changed.

The ban stood for three decades and left the sport to the amateurs, allowing an internationally recognised Springbok side to move to the forefront of the nation's sporting consciousness unopposed.

When another World Cup visited the country in 2010, this time in football, it provided a timely reminder of how far the nation had come in two decades. It was by no means settled, still trying to address the deeply ingrained problems caused by years of the apartheid regime, but it was on the way up. South Africa became the first African nation to host a football World Cup, a feat that would have been almost unthinkable eighteen years earlier when their apartheid-related ban from international football came to an end. Sport could so easily have slipped down the list of priorities for a country emerging from the depths of an apartheid regime. Few people would have blamed Mandela for ignoring the Rugby World Cup so soon after his inauguration, and many would have understood if the nation had stepped aside in 2004 as the bidding to host the 2010 football World Cup reached its climax.

The divides created by apartheid run deep, and remain part of the nation's consciousness. Effort and patience will be required to fully eradicate them, but South Africa's progress would have been much slower without football. On Robben Island it helped prisoners from warring factions to find a middle ground. It stopped the two leading political parties of today from separating further, and the mutual cooperation of these polarised groups has allowed the country to avoid additional and unnecessary obstacles.

The apartheid regime would have fallen with or without the Makana league, but the nation would not have been able to stand again as quickly in its absence.

Sport has been central in the country's rehabilitation. Fostering widespread and, more importantly, interracial support in 1995 for rugby, which had for so long been an exclusively white sport, ranks among Mandela's greatest achievements. The achievement of football's former outcasts in hosting the 2010 football World Cup so impeccably rebranded South Africa as a forward-thinking nation. Both tournaments have renewed the country internally as well as externally. The legacy of the Makana football league is wide-reaching; without football, South Africa would be a shadow of its present self.

Other books in the series:

IMAGINE THAT...
**THE HISTORY OF
FILM
REWRITTEN**

MICHAEL SELLS

IMAGINE THAT...
**THE HISTORY OF
TECHNOLOGY
REWRITTEN**

MICHAEL SELLS

IMAGINE THAT...
**THE HISTORY OF
MUSIC
REWRITTEN**

MICHAEL SELLS

If you enjoyed this book, here's a sample from *Imagine That ... Music*

Imagine that ...

MTV flops as music fans side with the radio star ... and hip-hop never reaches the mainstream

The legacy of Music Television divides opinion. For many, MTV breathed life into the music business. TV music show *Top of the Pops* was already a long-established institution in the UK before television producers in New York dreamt up round-the-clock music television. It made sense, there was demand – so why not supply? By adding a visual element to the music it challenged musicians to become more rounded performers. People already knew what the stars of the music business looked like, but now there was a chance for break-through acts to get their face known. For others MTV is merely a synonym for the prioritisation of image over musical content.

It's important to establish what MTV is. 'Music Television' is the obvious answer, but it's also now the wrong answer.

Officially, at least from a branding point of view, Music Television no longer exists, since the name was permanently abbreviated to 'MTV' in 2010. The television channel that launched on 1 August 1981 is no more, but the brand has developed into an empire. It has had arguably the biggest cultural impact of any television channel in history.

The argument goes that MTV was merely a vehicle to fame for the pretty people. Actually it became a test-ground for daring new looks. From Madonna's cropped wedding dress in her 'Like a Virgin' video to Michael Jackson's red leather jacket in 'Thriller', the videos helped to inspire fashion lines and fancy dress for years to come. Madonna and Michael Jackson were also two of the leading proponents of eye-catching videos, revelling in the chance to act out their lyrics.

It should be noted that music videos existed long before MTV and had received exposure through shows like *Top of the Pops*. MTV simply gave them a bigger platform. By the Nineties the varying genres of music video had become as well defined as the music. There were mini-epics like Guns N' Roses' wedding saga 'November Rain', animated adventures such as A-ha's pencil-sketched 'Take On Me' and even a Mad Hatter's tea party in Tom Petty's surreal 'Don't Come Around Here No More'. It has become increasingly easy for people in recent years to refer to MTV as a superficial music revolution – it was, after all, one based around image – but in the early days there was far greater creative content than people care to remember. There was also a defiant self-awareness that has been forgotten, perhaps even by the producers. The first track ever to air on MTV was a cover song

by a band called The Buggles: 'Video Killed the Radio Star'.

In 1990 a new media giant entered the scene and brought with it a revolutionary expansion of MTV's market. Sky TV changed the way people accessed television. Launched on a small scale, it went on to transform itself into a monopolising subscription service. For the first time viewers found themselves paying monthly to view the television that everyone was talking about. As the number of channels hosted by Sky grew, it started to sell subscriptions on a package basis. This meant that customers would purchase access to channels in blocks, i.e. sports, movies, and music. Forming the basis of the most desired packages, music channels boomed. There was a call for more channels and MTV was only too happy to oblige, dividing its output between numerous stations by genre. It was at this time that MTV changed irreversibly. It was soon joined by rival music channels. The phasing was seamless as MTV morphed from a one-channel brand into a multi-channel genre, signalling the beginning of the end for Music Television.

But after around a decade of continued growth, the music video became outdated. Or at least the means of viewing it did. As YouTube rose unstoppably to the top of the entertainment tree, artists were able to offer their music videos to fans on an unstoppable loop. It might not have spelled the end of music channels, but it certainly monopolised the market. Entertainment is an ever-changing business though, as MTV knew only too well, and so a rebrand was in order.

Suddenly music was bumped from the prime slots to be replaced by partially scripted reality-television shows, the antithesis of the original output of MTV. Channels dedicated to music videos still exist, but they have lost the commanding power they carried until the mid-Nineties. They no longer have the power to dictate which artists will be hits. Instead this power has been divided. Internet-based social networks and YouTube are driving the music business more than ever now. The power lies in the hands of the public. Editorial policy has been replaced by word of mouth. Whereas MTV offered budding stars the chance to get noticed by the public once they had a recording contract, YouTube allows users to gain exposure without backing, either financially or from the music business. The immediacy of the internet means that singers and songwriters can rise to fame in next to no time once they 'go viral'. The prime example of this is teen-sensation Justin Bieber. Gaining a large YouTube following after his mother had uploaded videos of him singing, the Canadian R&B star was spotted by talent scout Scooter Braun in 2007 aged just thirteen. His first album went multi-platinum, and by the age of eighteen Bieber was commanding enough power in the music business to sign fellow Canadian Carly Rae Jepson to his label. Naturally, Jepson soon started to top the charts herself. Stars that were once made on MTV no longer need

to impress television bosses to get known. Music has taken matters into its own hands.

The music business is an incredibly fluid one and most developments are temporary. MTV had more impact on it more than most, enjoying a heyday lasting nearly two decades. The changes it brought about shook the world of music, but what if the viewing public had shunned it when it debuted in the summer of 1981?

The MTV revolution brought a daring new element to the works of pop acts. Suddenly they needed to present themselves creatively through film as well song and dress. This limited many artists and liberated many others. Madonna, as we've seen, flourished amid the broadening of music media. There appeared to be good reason for this. Madonna already had an interest in cinema and her film career actually predates her music career by four years. She also developed a strong interest in fashion, reinventing her image on a number of occasions. These two elements combined with her musical talents to make her a more eclectic prospect than many of the acts she was up against. Rather than just watching a musician in a video, viewers would see a video-star in Madonna, someone who had tailored her act to suit the medium.

Without MTV and the music video, Madonna would have been deprived of the edge she had over many of her peers.

MTV played to her strengths and cemented her place in the public eye to a greater degree than her music and live performances alone would have done. Equally, middling artists of years gone by might have been propelled into the upper echelons of showbiz had MTV been in its pomp when they were recording.

It wasn't just those who embraced the cinematic element of MTV who prospered. The medium also promoted many exciting new genres of music, most notably rap and hip-hop. Two years before the birth of MTV, the now legendary Sugarhill Gang released a record featuring a brand-new sound. With their song 'Rappers Delight' they became the first band to achieve chart success with a rap single. It belonged to a much broader style of music known as hip-hop, originating

in the New York suburb of the Bronx. Despite being considered very much a novelty act at the time, the Sugarhill Gang were pioneering the most important genre of the next two decades – and just in time for MTV. Indeed, the rise of hip-hop coincided with the huge upturn in music videos on television. Originally hip-hop was predominantly the work of black performers – although some high-profile white performers have found success in the genre since, the Beastie Boys and Eminem for example. At the outset, it faced strong opposition from black-oriented radio stations, since much of the content of hip-hop was seen to present a negative image of black people. As such, without MTV to provide exposure for its stars, hip-hop would have faced an ongoing struggle to reach mainstream audiences.

Going back nearly three decades to the rise of Elvis Presley, music performed and embraced by black musicians was facing the same oppression that hip-hop was in the late 1970s and early 1980s. The role that MTV played in popularising hip-hop could have worked for other black genres such as the blues, had it existed at that time. The rise in black music was more than just a matter of gaining a share of the market – it was gaining a platform for the voice of an entire race. While hip-hop was by no means universally

embraced by black people, it paved the way for greater racial equality on television and in the mainstream media. When MTV first launched it took almost 60 videos for a non-white performer to feature, and even then it was a band featuring more white members than black. The video was 'Rat Race' by UK ska band The Specials. It was a stuttering start, but in time the racial make-up of MTV became far more representative of its viewers.

It's impossible to overestimate the effect that MTV has had on modern life. The changes that have shaped the channel in its long and varied history of programming have also shaped the world around us, for better or worse. To eradicate the MTV legacy would be to rewrite modern culture. This can be seen in the channel's change in programming. In the early days of the channel when music was king, the

content showed the celebrities of the time, not the effects of celebrity. The programmes that replaced the music have a strong following but they are indicative of a very different type of music fan. Shows such as *MTV Cribs*, for example, reveal a palpable change in attitude. This is a programme built solely around the concept of incredibly wealthy music stars and celebrities showing a camera crew around their mansions. This is not a new concept. *Through the Keyhole*, the cult game show from the 1980s and 1990s, identified and capitalised on the allure of voyeuristic content. Back then, though, it served a functional purpose: it was a guessing game that forced contestants to make links between celebs and their likely possessions. *MTV Cribs* just gawps slack-mouthed at rich people. As they show us around, there's rarely any mention of their creative work; instead all we get are tales of a rock and roll lifestyle and a hedonistic exist-ence. Although it's baffling that this has replaced the crea-tive content on a channel set up with the mission of provid-ing the world with extensive musical coverage, it's merely evidence of a television station providing its viewers with what they want.

This shouldn't be seen as MTV passively following trends. Yes, it responds to the desires of its viewers, but these are desires that MTV shaped years ago. Once the trailblazer of modern culture, it's now able to gently guide its loyal follow-ers down its own path. The channels that might once have been competitors have become supporting acts, reaffirming the validity of MTV with their presence. MTV has become self-perpetuating.

In the same way that hip-hop saw its rise aided by the station, the editorial power to alter music and society existed too. Once MTV was established as a popular medium, it gained the power to set trends, not just reflect them. When Music Television became MTV it was seen as a result of music videos losing popularity, which was partly true. It was also the result of demand for their increasingly popular non-musical television shows. Without the original Music Television there would be no MTV; and without MTV the excess of vacuous celebrity content would not exist, nor would we crave it. Nor would the celebrities whose lives make up the shows.

In 2011 the UK ratings body for radio, RAJAR (Radio Joint Audience Ratings), released figures showing that, after years of diminishing audiences for radio, there had been a shift. The ratings had started to head in the opposite direction. It was revealed that 47.2 million people were tuning into radio stations each week, the highest figures in just under two decades, proof that radio has remained relevant despite the onslaught of MTV. Rather than being killed off, the radio star was simply sent away to hide for a little while, the fans distracted by a bright, flashing alternative. MTV didn't cut radio adrift after all – music rose above the image and all that accompanies the MTV generation.

If MTV had failed to take off and radio had played on undisturbed, where would we be now? While MTV is no longer a compelling exhibition of contemporary musical acts, the role it played in the Eighties and Nineties aided the progression of music. Radio would not have triumphed in the absence of MTV. It would be weaker, deprived of the wider array of sounds introduced by Music Television, including but not limited to hip-hop. Live gigs and CD sales would have fallen away too. The channel was a stepping stone for music. The music business switched focus from radio to MTV as it has now towards YouTube and downloads. This is merely a matter of fad and fashion. The fact that MTV changed focus when YouTube and downloading began to threaten, instead of fighting in vain to continue its dominance of music, meant that music was able to progress organically into a new era. With its media power, MTV had the power to impede upcoming acts – but instead it chose to step aside.

Of all the challengers vying to provide music's prime platform, radio will always be the strongest, as it's the purveyor of music in its purest form. But music is a diverse art form and the introduction of new media only acts to strengthen it. By adapting to appeal to a broader spectrum of society via MTV, acts like Madonna made the music industry more inclusive, enabling fans to take more from music than they ever had. Video didn't kill the radio star – nothing ever will – but perhaps we should be thankful that it stepped aside when it did.